TAKE BACK THE TRUTH

Also by Joanna Manning

Is the Pope Catholic? A Woman Confronts Her Church

TAKE BACK THE TRUTH

Confronting Papal Power
and the Religious
Right

JOANNA MANNING

A Crossroad Book
The Crossroad Publishing Company
New York

The Crossroad Publishing Company
481 Eighth Avenue, New York, NY 10001

Printed in the United States of America

Library of Congress Cataloging-in-Publication Data

Manning, Joanna, 1943-
    Take back the truth / Joanna Manning.
      p. cm.
    Includes bibliographical references.
    ISBN 0-8245-1976-0 (alk. paper)
    1. Feminism – Religious aspects – Catholic Church. 2. Sexism in
religion. I. Title.
BX2347.8.W6 M36 2002
282 – dc21

                           2002004765

1 2 3 4 5 6 7 8 9 10   08 07 06 05 04 03 02

Contents

Preface

The issues of truth raised in this book are ones that relate to the heart as well as to the mind. Truth cannot be taught merely as a series of propositions. It fails to convince unless it is also lived. The truth I live is one informed by faith. My faith came to birth and was nurtured within the Roman Catholic community, but has since moved beyond denominational Christian boundaries.

Born and raised in England, I also worked in Italy and France, and I am now Canadian by adoption. For twenty-five years I have worked closely with colleagues in the United States on women's issues and church reform. I have lived with Africans in Africa and with refugees from Africa and Latin America in my own home. Thus I have some acquaintance with the global impact of the Catholic Church and the Christian right.

While I make no claim to universality, I hope this book bears traces of an authentic search for integrity that will resonate with others. In writing it, I have been supported by a shining cloud of witnesses both near and far. All over the world, courageous people are struggling to sustain faith in the future and to speak the truth to power within churches and society.

The time we live in is fraught with ambiguity, obscurity, and danger. "We ride our horses," as an ancient Zen saying expressed it, "along the edge of a sword." A new but fragile truth of global solidarity is emerging in this postmodern twenty-first century, but it is under grave threat from a resurgence of religious fanaticism and fundamentalism. This book challenges the current reactionary trends within Christianity in the hope of ensuring a safer world for all our children.

Special thanks to my research assistant, Carole Thompson, and to Rosemary Ganley and Jane Koster, skilled textual readers who also provided me with many helpful ideas and insights.

ONE

What Is Truth?

On February 13, 1991, I spent the night in jail. It was one of the worst experiences of my life, one that I fervently hope I will never have to endure again. It was Ash Wednesday, the first day of Lent. Since the fall, I had been part of a group formed by the Catholic Worker Community of Toronto to plan nonviolent resistance to the Gulf War. Canada's prime minister, Brian Mulroney, had caved in to pressure from President George H. W. Bush and committed Canadians to support the United States–led force without seeking the consent of the people through their elected representatives in Parliament.

At the time, I was head of religious education at Monsignor Johnson Catholic High School in Toronto and had been leading a group of students and teachers every Friday morning in a silent public demonstration against the mounting hostilities. When we first started the action, the passing motorists had been supportive, honking their horns, smiling and waving. However, as soon as the decision was made to commit Canadian troops to the bombing of Iraq, the public reception of our protest changed to anger. All of a sudden, we were seen as a threat to Mulroney's campaign to sell the war as a patriotic enterprise in which "our boys and girls" were risking their lives to defend the world from Saddam Hussein, a cruel and wicked tyrant. Control by the West of Iraq's oil supplies, the real reason for the hostilities, faded into the background.

This was a striking example of how easy it is for the power of truth and integrity to be changed into truths manufactured by power. In media critic Noam Chomsky's phrase, the Canadian government had "manufactured consent" for the war, supported by a compliant media that portrayed the bombing of Iraq and the "Desert Storm" campaign as a glorified video game played with "smart bombs" that would cause only "collateral damage." The almost instantaneous change of attitude of the drivers who witnessed our protest from week to week

1

was a frightening example of how quickly such "contagious" consent could be manufactured.

The Catholic Worker group had decided to enact a symbolic Ash Wednesday protest at the headquarters of the Conservative Party in central Toronto. In keeping with the liturgical theme of the day, we planned to pray on the street outside and cross ourselves with ashes before scattering them on the steps of the building.

I was one of the leaders of the third group, due to meet at 6:00 p.m. Just as we were in the process of scattering the ashes, a police cruiser drew up at the curb. Two officers jumped out. "You're under arrest for public mischief," they said. They handcuffed my colleague Jim Loney and me and bundled us into the back of the squad car. Once at the station we were fingerprinted and photographed. They sat us down in the office for a while, and then the senior officer came back and told us that they would give us a choice. "We can either call in a justice of the peace now, and you can swear an oath that you will not take part in any future demonstrations against the Gulf War, or we'll charge you with public mischief and you'll spend the night in a cell and appear in court tomorrow."

At that moment, I remembered the news clips I had watched the night before our demonstration when the "smart bombs" launched by the allies had fallen on an underground shelter in Baghdad, killing all the women and children who had taken refuge there. At the time, it seemed that this war about Western access to cheap oil in the Persian Gulf was going to claim the lives of an increasing number of innocent civilians. I therefore decided that to renounce my democratic right to peaceful protest was too high a price to pay for my freedom, and so I refused the offer of the release.

As we drove west along the highway toward the women's jail located in Rexdale, I realized with an eerie sense of recognition that we were taking the same route that I took to get to school every morning. It occurred to me that I could possibly get fired from teaching as a result of this action, so this could be one of the last times I would take this road out to the west end toward my school.

The patrol car stopped at the side entrance to the jail. It looked from a distance like a large factory. We drove in, and I was deposited at the front entrance. "Take off your earrings, your watch, and all your personal belongings and put them in this plastic bag," the female guard at the reception desk said. Then she took me to an open cubicle to the side of the entrance. "Take off all your clothes," she said.

I stripped and then she walked all around me inspecting my body. "Now bend over." I felt a finger go into my anus and a few seconds later into my vagina. As I bent down and looked between my legs, I saw a male guard pass by, with full view of what was happening. By that time I was feeling so traumatized I had lost any inclination to protest this additional humiliation.

"Here, put these clothes on." I was handed a pair of outsized striped pajamas and a rough pair of socks. "Come this way." I shuffled out behind her.

We came into a large, brightly lit circular area with concrete floor and walls. All around were the cells, with two bunk beds in each, four women to a cell. The guards opened one of the cages and threw a mattress onto the floor. The door clanged shut behind me. My mattress took up most of the empty floor space. There was an open toilet near the bars and when I lay down, my head was about four inches from the toilet bowl.

I slept very little that night. The guards played loud music and talked the whole time. I was exhausted but also felt as tense as a coiled spring from trying to keep hold of a modicum of sanity in the midst of this battering of my psychic strength. My most immediate worry was a very practical concern: How would I ever be able to empty my bowels in the immediate presence of four other people and in full view of the whole block? I prayed that the urge would come on me while it was still dark and I would not have to perform this unavoidable bodily function in full daylight. Unfortunately it was daylight the next morning when I had to sit on the toilet and then wipe myself in public.

I could see one star in the sky through a tiny window at the back of the cell. Somehow it kept me attached by an invisible umbilical cord to the rest of the world. I thought of other women who had been imprisoned, particularly Innu women, natives of Sheshasheit in Labrador who had been jailed the previous summer for protesting the low-level flying of NATO jets over their land.[1] I had spent some time with them, living in tents in their summer encampment by the banks of the Labrador River. I felt that this night represented the culmination of a series of small steps I had taken which had now carried me beyond the boundaries of the status quo. I would now be definitively marked as an outsider, a felon.

Early next morning as we were being awakened, a guard came to the door calling my name. "Manning! Manning! Here are your clothes. You're going to court this morning." I dressed hastily and was led to an elevator packed with other inmates. We were then placed — about forty people together — in a large holding cell. A few minutes later, a trolley cart was pushed through the door with eggs, toast, and some large containers of tea and coffee.

About half the group rushed forward and fell on the food. A scuffle broke out. I initially held back, but decided I would have to appear somewhat assertive, otherwise I would be picked on as a neophyte. I tried to appear confident as I went up to get food, but I was afraid of being singled out. I found that there were no eggs left. I took a couple of pieces of toast and filled a cup with coffee and found a place on the floor against the back wall. An attractive young woman sitting a few feet away beckoned to me to sit next to her. "Here," she said, offering me an egg, "take one of my eggs — I don't need two."

We were lined up and handcuffed together in groups of eight. Then we were loaded into a paddy wagon bolted together on benches in the back. As we sped along the highway my companion Debbie, who had given me the egg, was sitting next to me and smoking. Every time she lifted her right hand to take a drag on the cigarette, up went my left hand as well.

As we were unloaded, we were told that we could talk to our lawyer or to the duty counsel who represents all those who do not have a lawyer. Shortly afterward, my name was called out because a lawyer had arrived to represent me. Don Schmidt, president of my teachers union, had made some hasty phone calls and arranged for the teachers union to retain a lawyer on my behalf.

As I was being led into the dock in handcuffs, I saw Don and other friends sitting in the court, which lifted my spirits immensely. The Crown argued for bail of $1000 and a three-hundred-meter limit to my access to Canadian or American government buildings. The judge granted bail without conditions.

A few months later on the date set for my trial, many of my students sought and received permission to accompany me to court. The courtroom was packed with young people sitting on the floor and in the aisles. But after a brief deliberation with the Crown prosecutor, the judge announced that the charges had been dropped, and Jim Loney and I were free to go. Some measure of the truth about the Gulf War was beginning to emerge and serious questions had been raised about Canadian involvement. The so-called truths propagated by the Western powers were beginning to be exposed as falsehoods, especially the report of a notorious incident in which Iraqi troops allegedly unplugged the electrical connections from incubators in a Kuwait hospital. This outrageous charge had proved to be a media invention.

THE MANUFACTURING OF CONSENT to the questionable use of political or military power through a manipulation of truth is not confined to the secular sphere. It has proved to be one of the features of the papacy of John Paul II. The past thirty years in the Catholic Church have seen a return to ultramontanism, or excessive adulation of papal power, that many thought had been discredited by the Second Vatican Council. The diversity of lay experience and insight, which could act as a healthy counterbalance and challenge to the narrow clerical world of priests and bishops, has been carefully channeled into "new movements" such as Opus Dei and Human Life International. These groups are "lay" only in name, because in practice they are carefully supervised by the priests and bishops who lead them. Rome now holds up these new movements as evidence of resurgence of lay vigor in the church.

It has become evident to me that both the Western media's suppression of the truth of the Gulf War and the Vatican's use of authoritarian groups within the church to suppress internal dissent constitute an example of what the French philosopher René Girard calls "mimetic violence."[2] Mimesis means a symbolic re-enactment. "Mimetic violence" refers to symbolic or concrete acts of violence which happen as a result of the collective will of a group that has been manipulated into or caught up into a mass frenzy. The root of mimetic violence lies within a desire to conform, to belong, or to be on the winning side. It is not hard to convince the mass of people that they have a common enemy. The frenzy of mass fear or hatred is contagious and spreads rapidly. Once aroused, the group needs a scapegoat to function as an outlet for its fears or hatred. The collective will then demands that the scapegoat be actually or symbolically killed or exiled, so that the group's fear of contamination may be purged. In the case of the Gulf War, Saddam Hussein had become the target of its hate. No matter that Saddam Hussein was once the West's ally. Truth is the first victim of mimetic violence. When a group gets caught into this collective hysteria, the frenzy of conformity demands that dissenters be silenced. If they persist, the collective violence of the mob becomes displaced and attacks the voices of dissent.

Within the Catholic Church, truth has now become the victim of the pressures of mass conformity and loyalty to the pope. Adolescents are particularly susceptible to this pressure to conform. Papal Youth Days, such as those to be held in Toronto in July 2002, are carefully designed to maximize the mimetic power of the papacy. The manufacturing of consent to the conservative agenda of the Vatican is concealed behind the hype and hoopla of the mass rally. Even the Stations of the Cross are presented as mass spectacle, not unlike the Super Bowl. The complexities of the gospel message are neatly packaged and presented in a fast-food, "McDonalds"-type question-and-answer formula, for easy consumption and instant gratification. Any expression of dissent is treated as disloyalty.

The past thirty years have witnessed a relentless attack on internal dissent within the Catholic Church. Theological debate of any consequence has been all but silenced, and creative Catholic thinkers have been forced or have chosen to move outside the walls of Catholic universities into the more welcoming and creative context of liberal Protestant or secular universities and colleges. Attacks on feminists, abortion clinics, gays and lesbians and others targeted by the Vatican and by Protestant fundamentalists as responsible for society's ills are tacitly if not overtly sanctioned. Enquiry into the Catholic Church's role in the Holocaust has been brushed under the carpet, while anti-Semitic popes such as Pius IX and Pius XII have been placed on the fast track to sainthood. Even the horrendous revelations of sexual abuse by Catholic clergy all over the world have been the subject of obfuscation and denial, and the symptoms of crisis within the Catholic priesthood, manifested in recent pedophilia and sexual abuse scandals, have been explained by blaming the victims or the modern world. None of its leaders is calling the church to face the truth about itself.

The time has come to take back the truth.

"WHAT IS TRUTH?" demanded Pontius Pilate of Jesus. The question was posed after Jesus had been handed over to Pilate by the Sanhedrin for judgment and sentencing. This book explores the implications of Jesus' answer to Pilate's question.

The power to seek, to name, and to live by truth is one of the cornerstones of human existence. The appropriation and the misappropriation of truth in the service of domination and violence affects almost every aspect of religion, politics, economics, and culture in the contemporary world. Violence in the name of a particular interpretation of truth, especially religious truth, is still a major factor in global conflict. The scapegoating of dissenting opinion and the desire to violently suppress the truth it represents continue to infect the internal workings of the Catholic Church. But at the heart of this storm, in the eye of the hurricane, the still small voice of the Spirit of Christ is calling out, trying to take back the truth. The Paraclete, or Advocate, the Spirit of Truth, is using the voices of the victims of violence to call the church to change.

Convictions about the nature of truth, the power to name the truth, and the relationship of truth to love are part of the personal and the political realities which the human community in each succeeding generation is called to articulate and live. To reach maturity, each of us has to continually search for, discover, and commit ourselves to our emerging truth. What our truth is and how we respond to it will determine our identity and how we live. Postmodernism, also known as deconstruction, has questioned the underlying objectivity of knowledge and truth in the West that has hitherto been accepted as universally applicable. It has exposed the fact that the content of this knowledge has been contained in a small number of "great" texts, or overarching metanarratives,[3] interpreted only by a privileged minority.

The brief conversation between Jesus and Pilate about truth has powerful implications for this postmodern dialogue about truth. Anticipating a simple yes or no answer, Pilate opens the interrogation by asking Jesus if he is the king of the Jews. But Jesus does not give a direct answer. He appears not to take Pilate's question at its face value. He opens up the question by attempting to find out more about the background, motivation, and context of his interrogator. "What is the origin and context of this enquiry?" Jesus asks. "Is this your own question, or is it one that has been put into your mouth by others?"

Jesus is deconstructing Pilate's question. He is approaching it with what, in postmodern terms, is called a "hermeneutic of suspicion."[4] In other words, the meaning of the question cannot be neatly assumed at its literal or face value. The true meaning will emerge only after the perspective and the power of the one who poses the question have been analyzed. According to postmodernism, the interpretation or naming of reality contains a desire to exercise power over that reality. So within the power of naming lies a power to control, and if necessary, to resort to violence to maintain the power of naming.[5]

Postmodernism has exposed the suppression of differences and the layers of class, gender, and race domination that have supported the privilege and dominance of the wealthy over the poor, of men over women, of heterosexual over homosexual, and of whites over other races. The great work of postmodernism has been to deconstruct these layers, expose the structures of oppression that support them, and open up the field to voices that have previously been suppressed.[6]

The Catholic Church is not the only religious institution that claims the exclusive right to truth. The resurgence in Protestant and Muslim fundamentalism has brought other religious players onto the stage of the global theater, each claiming to speak directly for God. The events of September 11, 2001, demonstrated this in stark reality. In juxtaposition to religious fundamentalism is the post-Enlightenment, post-Holocaust, postmodern, post-Western world of today: a world where truth is now viewed as historically and culturally conditioned and therefore always incomplete and continually in evolution. It is a world that has lived through several genocides enacted by religious or political authority in the name of truth. It no longer accepts that there can exist an objective, static body of knowledge defined by those in power. A world that has lived through the Holocaust no longer accepts the authority of anyone who claims to possess the truth in a neutral or value-free way. The postmodern world has seen the horrendous results of the dogmatic and allegedly objective and scientific schema of "truths" uttered by Nazis about Jews. It has seen the catastrophic results of the "truths" about women as defined by men, about blacks as defined by whites, and about sexual love as defined by celibates. At the onset of this third millennium, the voices of the victims of all of these "truths" are slowly but surely being acknowledged.

PILATE, LIKE SO MANY in power who feel threatened by the unsettling questions posed by victims of the ruling structures, is almost flippantly caustic in his response to Jesus. "Do you take me for a Jew!" "In other words," he seems to be saying, "I didn't initiate this whole episode — your own religious leaders did. So don't try to put words into my mouth. I've been around long enough to recognize an agitator when I encounter one. But," he cautions Jesus, "don't you ever forget who is in charge here and that people handed you over to me for their final solution." After Pilate has tried to settle the issue of Jesus' power with a resort to his own authority, he poses a direct question to Jesus: "So what have you done?"

One of the key issues of today is the relationship of truth to power. Pilate's response to Jesus' enquiry is typical of those who resort to power to settle an issue. He reminds Jesus that he, the Roman, is the one doing the defining of the status quo, not Jesus, the Jew who has been colonized by the superior imperial and cultured empire. Rome has spoken. Rome's truth comes down from above, and it is transmitted from God, represented by those who have power, at the end of a sword or a gun or through burning at the stake, or dropping a bomb if necessary. Is this the truth that Jesus came to speak? Jesus also claimed to speak truth with authority, but it was not an authority invested in him by an external or a violent power. Jesus never sought to manufacture consent to his truth. To those who had eyes to see, he lived the truth in all its integrity.

In order to analyze the relationship of truth to power, it is necessary to ask some key questions. The questions center around who gets to define the truth, whose truth are they defining, and what effect this has on others who may be either included or marginalized by their definition. Is there only one version of truth, as the Catholic hierarchy, for example, insists, or are there many versions of truth, dependent on the vantage point of the one doing the defining and the effect this definition has on others? And is it right that a small group of people get to define the truth for the rest of the human race?

Can truth exist within a diversity of interpretation? According to the hierarchical understanding of truth favored in the Catholic Church since it absorbed the governing structures of Pilate's Roman Empire, most definitely not. Pure truth is found at the top of a pyramid of the church's ascending power. Those who exist at the top live in a purified zone, where the truth is unpolluted by a diversity of viewpoints or life. The most polluted version of truth, the most relative, is found at the bottom. And the lower truth descends from the top of the pyramid, the more it gets distorted. So the "simple faithful" (that definition of lay people so beloved of Cardinal Josef Ratzinger, the head of the Catholic Church's Congregation for the Doctrine of the Faith) at the bottom of the heap cannot be disturbed by allowing them to dabble in speculation. Theirs is but to obey, perhaps to pray and, most certainly, to pay.

This hierarchical interpretation of truth is being questioned today. Those at the bottom of the pyramid will no longer submit to having

their lives defined for them. Indeed, the whole hierarchical structure
of the pyramid itself is being called in question. The task before the
Catholic Church today is to remold the pyramid of hierarchical authority — slow and painful though the work may be — into a circle
of inclusive consensus. A circle of love, a circle that embraces and
celebrates diversity. A circle defined not by relativism, but by rela-
tionality and connectedness. Like the earth itself, the truth is round
and interconnected. All truths lead into each other. Truth is circular,
ambivalent, partial, tentative, and evolving.

Jesus' answers to Pilate's questions about truth are elliptical. He
curves away from a direct answer about his authority, and then back
toward Pilate's first question. He states that, yes, he is indeed a king
and the power in this kingdom belongs to those who speak and listen
to truth. And then comes Pilate's famous riposte: "What is truth?"
Did Pilate, as some commentators suggest, then walk away with a
shrug, not giving Jesus time to answer, or did Jesus simply stand
silent before his inquisitor? We shall never know for sure.

But Pilate's questions to Jesus echo down the ages for those who
have tried to follow Jesus' way, truth, and life. Who are you? What
have you done? What is your truth?

JESUS LIVED AND PREACHED a paradoxical and ambivalent truth that
was found primarily in loving. The opposite of truth in the service of
power is truth in the service of love. This is the power of the truth
that Jesus came to witness to and for which he gave his life. Truth in
the service of love seeks to widen the circle of inclusivity by enlarging
its boundaries. Outsiders are not a threat to the integrity of the circle;
they simply effect a change in the definition of its boundaries. Even
Jesus had to learn about this and enlarge his own boundaries, and it
was a woman, a woman who was very much an outsider, who taught
him this lesson. In the fifteenth chapter of Matthew's Gospel, there
is a striking story of a Canaanite woman and her daughter, who is
described as "possessed by a demon."

The woman and her daughter are alone. This suggests that she
might have been a single parent, a single parent with an incapaci-
tated daughter. This is a double marginalization: two women in a
patriarchal male world, two women who are considered racially and
ritually unclean. This mother must also have heard many times over
the prevailing religious wisdom that the fact that her child was not
normal was a sign that she had done something displeasing to God.

Initially this woman shouted out to Jesus and the disciples as they passed along the road: "Son of David! Take pity on me and my daughter because she is possessed." She met with hard looks and hard hearts. Not once, but three times, Jesus refused her cry for help. The first time he took no notice; the second time he told her that he was "sent only to the lost sheep of Israel" — in other words that she and her daughter were not included in his healing mission and she should leave him alone. The third time she persisted in crying out, Jesus was positively rude: "It is not right to take the children's food and throw it to the dogs," he snapped.

But this woman didn't let Jesus off the hook. "But even the dogs eat the leftovers from under the table," she shot back. You can almost feel that Jesus' own understanding of the truth is shifting dramatically with this woman's intervention. His experience of his tradition came face to face with the desire, the urgent cry of the God of the marginalized, that Jesus suddenly recognized in the voice of this woman. This suggests to me that Jesus learned from this woman. The limitations of his human understanding of his mission were expanded by contact with the racially marginalized. This woman taught Jesus to transgress the boundaries of his religion. Later, the movement of Jesus' community would follow this trajectory when they decided to include gentiles in the church without first submitting them to the ritual of circumcision. The church's initial impetus, modeled on many incidents like this one where Jesus reacts to the Canaanite woman, was toward a painful widening of its boundaries to include the excluded.

Jesus invited the religious authorities to completely revamp their version of truth by looking at the truth from God's perspective. For God, the truth is not about what we believe or how well we keep the commandments. It is about how we love. This reveals that at the heart of the gospel, or good news, at the heart of Jesus' truth is love, a love that goes beyond an adherence to religious orthodoxy.

Whenever Jesus spoke about the truth, it was not in the form of an abstract dogma, but in the context of life and experience. Jesus' truth is neither dispassionate nor neutral: it strikes to the heart of the person like a fire between the marrow and the bone. "I am the way, the truth, and the life" (John 14:6). Truth cannot be separated from the way it is lived. It does not float in the abstract. Truth is not found in a set of definitions in a catechism; it is found along the way as we walk our path through life. The truth is in the walk, the truth is in the life, and the truth is in the loving.

The absence of a right relationship between truth and love is at the center of the Catholic Church's dysfunction today. Obsessed with purity, with the boundaries of orthodoxy, and with defining and imposing its version of the truth on people at any cost, the institutional Catholic Church has lost sight of the fundamental principle of love. It has become so obsessed with control that it is neglecting its primary mission of compassion and healing. The Catholic Church, in its obsession with control, has lost sight of Jesus of Nazareth.

The Catholic Church today has fallen back onto "manufacturing consent" to truths that no longer touch people in a life-giving way. Catholics have withdrawn their consent from the truths the church teaches on contraception, homosexual relationships, divorce, and Sunday Mass obligations by simply abandoning the practice of them in their lives. Surveys show that the majority of Catholics also disagree with the hierarchy's ban on married clergy and women priests, both "truths" that have been relentlessly hammered home in the papacy of John Paul II, under threat of excommunication. The increasingly severe penalties attached to dissent from the hierarchy's teaching and the public humiliation of dissenters are all directed toward the manufacturing of consent among the simple faithful. But most of the faithful are not so simple anymore.

There are still some Catholics for whom the authority of the pope and the hierarchy remains unquestioned. In speaking with conservative Catholics about, for example, pedophilia among Catholic clergy, I often ask them: "What do you think that Jesus would say or do about this situation?" This question is sometimes met with incredulity. "What has Jesus of Nazareth to do with this?" is the response. Then they will tell me that the problem has arisen because priests are not listening to and obeying the church (meaning the pope and bishops). The hierarchy has codified all the rules about compulsory celibacy; they have all the answers to every question about how it is to be observed. The problem is that people won't obey the rules. If they did, the church would get along just fine and go about its business without such annoying distractions from its mission to convert the world. The church already has the whole truth on every other issue from contraception to cloning, and it has been codified, compiled, and distilled in canon law and in thousands of papal exhortations, encyclicals, and letters housed in the Vatican Library, the repository of truth for all time.

In their view, the sexual abuse scandals in the church are the result of individual, not systemic, problems. These scandals have been blown out of all proportion by a hostile secular media bent on destroying the Catholic Church. The media have allegedly exaggerated these stories because most of the media is under the control of secular humanists hostile to the church. There is nothing wrong with the system if only the individuals within it would shape up. This version of the truth is one which regards the truth as universal, objective, certain, and historically unchanging. It is one that is derived from a rigid mindset that is blind to its own limitations and particularities.

Jesus' TRUTHS were revealed in stories he told which were drawn from his own life experience. He discovered and taught the truth in stories about sowing seeds, about family quarrels over inheritance, about women looking for coins. But those who profess to teach in his name today are far removed from life, family, kitchens, and the earth. It is time for the church to recover the wisdom of the earth and the kitchen table. This year I have been fixing up my garden and planting new perennials at the front and the back of the house. The garden needs a lot of tender loving care, especially in the long, hot summers here in Toronto. Each night when it doesn't rain I water the garden. I hear the sound of the water spraying out from the hand-held hose, and I think of the water from the rock — the water of life that feeds our parched souls.

Sometimes God graces us with the gentle mist of light droplets; sometimes with a torrential flood that has to be carefully handled or it will overwhelm us. Does the pope or any of his cardinals ever water their gardens? There is a magnificent formal garden at the back of the Vatican. I once walked there with my children many years ago when I visited Rome. Hidden in one of the bushes in the Vatican gardens we came across a mother cat with her brood of kittens who ran out to play with us in the sunshine. Would the pope ever find those kittens and stop to play with them?

I sometimes wonder if the pope has ever changed a diaper or been peed on by a toddler who hasn't quite mastered the art of getting to the bathroom on time. I recall an occasion many years ago when a priest friend came to visit us. He took off his jacket and laid it over one of the chairs in the living room. My son, who was being toilet-trained at the time, curled up and went to sleep in the jacket. When he got up, a dark stain was visible where he had been lying. Horrors! He had had an accident right in the middle of a Jesuit jacket! The priest in question was very understanding and took it all in good spirit. He is now one of the chief astronomers at the Vatican observatory, and I wonder if he still wears that jacket as he gazes at the stars.

I think that Jesus probably got peed on by a number of toddlers in the course of his ministry. He loved children, and they were attracted to him. He was approachable enough that they would have felt confident enough to scramble up into his lap even though the apostles tried to shoo them away (Mark 10:13–16). All of this life experience spilled over into Jesus' teachings and illuminated the truths he told. His truths were drawn from daily life, the life and the loving of real people, the vines and the gardens they tended, the loaves of bread they baked, the neighbors who woke them up in the middle of the night.

One of the other reasons the Catholic Church is now foundering is because its leaders have lost the connection with the truth of a life lived exuberantly and love poured out unconditionally. They live in an airtight bubble, immune from soiled diapers, digging in the garden, and baking bread. Mandatory celibacy removes Catholic priests from the blood, sweat, and tears of intimate relationships, and the truths that flow from the living of these.

How did we end up so far from living the loving that is the truth of the gospel? Why does the pope seem so obsessed with a truth that controls people rather than sets them free? The Word and Wisdom uttered and lived by Jesus were transformative. It is being faithful to the Way as well as to the Word, the doing of the truth rather than just defining it, that transforms. It is the one who is faithful to the living of the Word who has the power to announce it, not the one whose preaching is fenced around by rigid rules that domesticate the power of the gospel. True prophets enter into history and transgress its boundaries by proclaiming freedom to those captive within religious or social bonds, often engendering social or religious conflict that ends with exile or death.[7]

The gospel according to the church, it seems, is no longer meant to trouble or upset. The Catholic hierarchy seems to believe that the power of the gospel to shock and scandalize was only relevant to the initial preaching of Jesus. The Eucharist, the re-enactment of Jesus' paschal life, is no longer dangerous or disturbing. It is not necessary now to return again and afresh to the person and message of Jesus because, according to this view, all that has been sewn up neatly by the pope. This idolizing of authority as vested in the person of the pope, which has drawn many Catholics back into its orbit once again over the past thirty years, has created a new empire of the church. It has reinstated a church modeled on an image of Caesar's empire, which has become an end in itself rather than the means to salvation. The result is that the Catholic hierarchy has to resort to increasingly violent means to enforce their version of the truth.

In the fifth chapter of Mark's Gospel, Jesus crosses to the other side of Lake Galilee, to a wild place called Gerasa. A man possessed by a whole crowd of evil spirits, whose torments caused him to mutilate his own body, meets him. Others had tried to tie the man down in shackles, but he kept breaking free. He lived among graves, in a burial ground. As Jesus stepped off the boat, the man cried out in fear: "What do you want with us, Jesus of Nazareth?" (Mark 5:1–8). Today, there are many inside churches who are wandering in the burial grounds of the past. They mutilate their spirits in order to conform to what the authorities tell them, but the shackles of the certainties imposed on them do not contain the truth they are searching for. Each succeeding age must meet Jesus anew.

The Greek word for truth, *aletheia*, means literally "to stop forgetting." To search for truth means to remember where we came from and whose way we follow. In their anxiety to force uncritical submission to their version of truth, the lawmakers of the Catholic Church have forgotten the heart of the message of Jesus. That is why their efforts lack credibility.

THE TWENTIETH CENTURY has seen Christian churches in general, and the Catholic Church in particular, embroiled in an internal struggle that goes to the heart and soul of the gospel message. It is a conflict between power and service. This is a struggle that has haunted the church ever since the time of Constantine, when it inherited the mantle of power of the Roman Empire. It has formed a central contradiction of the papacy of John Paul II, which has seen an attempt to use the church's power to rule in an unprecedented way. The powerful myth of papal authority, and the lure of Caesaropapism,[8] which this has generated in the Catholic Church, has caused many Catholics to forget that the truth of the gospel is love.

The lure of this authority is such that it can and does impose deceit and denial in the interest of its own self-preservation. It is only in recent times that the children who were sexually abused by representatives of the church have found, as adults, a safe and impartial place, often only under the protection of the law in a civil court, in which to tell their stories. Even those closest to the victims of this abuse had become trapped in a hypnotic spell exerted by church authority and rendered blind and deaf to the victims of the church's covert violence.

When the first revelations of sexual abuse of children and youth by clergy came out in the media in the United States and Canada in the 1980s, some heartrending stories surfaced of the reactions of the parents of the victims. Mothers and fathers refused to believe the stories their children were bringing home and sometimes even punished them for saying such disgraceful things about priests. This denial was often aided and abetted by the social and community services and by members of the victims' extended families and parishes. In Newfoundland, once a very Catholic province of Canada, the majority of people who hold government jobs have been educated by nuns or priests. As a result, when the victims of clerical sexual abuse first tried to approach the civil authorities with their stories, they received precious little sympathy and even less serious attention. No good Catholic could believe that Father could have done anything remotely resembling a sexual assault on a child. When I visited Newfoundland in 1989 to talk with some of the victims, one young man told me about the reaction he got when he tried to tell a visiting bishop about the sexual advances made by one of the priests in the parish. When word of his complaint to the bishop got out, the following Sunday he was hauled outside and beaten up by two members of the Knights of Columbus. So threatening was the power of truth on the lips of this victim, that those who served the power of the church felt they had to forcibly repress and restrain it.

The enforcement of conformity, the manufacturing of consent to truth as presently promulgated by the hierarchy of the Catholic Church has become increasingly violent in the last twenty-five years under John Paul II. Though not as extreme as the measures adopted by the former Taliban regime in Afghanistan, recent reactionary developments in the Catholic Church have run in parallel tracks to the resurgence of fundamentalist movements in Protestantism, Judaism, and Islam. The new links between Catholic papal fundamentalism and Protestant biblical fundamentalism will be examined in chapter 4.

In major segments of all of the mainstream Western religions, there has been a retreat into a rigidity of doctrine, authoritarian rule, and ruthless application of the law. Excommunication, and the threat of excommunication, which since the Second Vatican Council had been thought to be a thing of the past, has come back into usage within the Catholic Church. This is a fearful reaction to postmodernism's deconstruction of truth and a descent into what is viewed as pure relativity where anything goes. This fear of the postmodern world can be attributed to the rise of feminism and the threat this presents to patriarchal control in all spheres. Religions that hold to the maleness of God as a bedrock creed, on which the superiority of the male gender and men's right to rule is constructed, feel themselves under intense pressure from the global rise to consciousness of equality-seeking women. The unholy alliance at the United Nations of the Vatican and like-minded conservative Muslim states intent on blocking women's control over their bodies and sexuality is evidence of this.

This fear of the disintegration of a carefully constructed world of male dominance has fueled a new movement to curtail freedom of thought and expression, especially on women's issues. Little do the Catholic hierarchy realize that the Catholic Church no longer commands the power of the days of its medieval apogee, when popes such as Gregory VII and Innocent III claimed the power to make and unmake emperors. The contemporary tightening of centralized control merely demonstrates an abject failure to convince the rest of the world of the credibility of their truth by means of persuasion rather than coercion. Islamic fundamentalists and their Catholic and Protestant counterparts have fallen back onto control through fear. For Protestant fundamentalists this fear is that of eternal damnation in hell. For Catholics, it is the fear of reprisal by excommunication, which amounts to the same fate, because if a Catholic dies excommunicate, he or she is condemned to hell anyway.

THOSE WHO HAVE a compulsive need to impose their version of absolute and unchanging truth on others manifest two profoundly disturbing traits. One is a proclivity to demonize those who do not agree or fit the definition. The other is the need to depend on some external authority for validation of the truth. This produces a dangerous adulation and unquestioning, blind obedience to authority. I remember a discussion about ten years ago with a religious Brother who had been appointed to help out with the chaplaincy program at the high school where I was head of religion. He seemed utterly convinced that the pope's teaching on women priests was right and should be obeyed without question. "What if the next pope changes the teaching?" I asked him. "Will you still hold on to your present opinion?" "Oh, no," he replied. "If the pope told me to change it I would." "Just like that?" I replied. "Oh yes — whatever the pope says is always right" was his response. Such attitudes leave the church vulnerable to fascism and its uncritical worship of power as truth.

Another characteristic of the worship of power as truth is the cult of personality that swirls around an authoritarian leader. Pope John Paul's pontificate has fostered a cult of personality around the pope. A consummate communicator, the pope has seized on the unprecedented opportunity offered by the modern media to make his views heard and his presence felt all over the globe. Papal Youth Days, for example, are designed to draw Catholic youth into renewed conformity to conservative Catholicism.

The air of unreality, of the contrived and carefully controlled display like a circus performance that characterizes the papal World Youth Days, also clings to the cadre of elitist lay movements that have been promoted under John Paul II. The doyen of the "New Religious Movements," as they are known in Rome, is Opus Dei. It was founded in the 1930s in fascist Spain, but was previously on the margins of the church. In the past twenty years, Opus Dei, as well as Communion and Liberation, the Neo-Catechumenate, and the Legionaries of Christ, have all received papal endorsement. Other movements working in a more focused way against feminism, such as Human Life International, Priests for Life, and the Catholic Family and Human Rights Institute, have also found favor with Rome. Each pursues a vision of a Catholicism that is theologically reactionary and highly hierarchical and authoritarian in structure. They exemplify the "holier than thou" mentality of a cult, founded on what they view as absolute possession of the truth, an unswerving devotion to its promulgation, and a mission to crush dissenting opinions. Papal encouragement of these Catholic sects is a dangerous move, one that runs contrary to the true catholicity of the church.[9]

Hand in hand with the rise of conservative Catholic cults, the past thirty years have seen a proliferation of papal teaching aimed at reasserting the church's control over sexuality and the family. This has coincided with a promulgation of a "family values" agenda among evangelical Protestants, which has been fueled by a desire to return to traditional patriarchal control over the family and over women. The private zone of morality, long thought to have been out of the bounds of regulation in modern secular democracies, has become a major area of contention in the public zone of legislation. The rise of the religious right as a political force in the United States has coincided with John Paul II's attempt to make the Catholic Church into a force on the international stage.

Under the presidency of George W. Bush, the interests of these two conservative forces of church and state have converged at national and international levels. Under the presidency of Ronald Reagan and his successor, George H. W. Bush, the goal of the Rome-Washington axis was to engage papal support for the defeat of communism in Eastern Europe and the crushing of Catholic liberation theology in Latin America. Once that goal had been met and the Berlin Wall had fallen in 1989, John Paul's attention in the 1990s swung to the defeat of what he believed was the next greatest threat to humanity: the global rise of the feminist movement. Initially, during the years of the Clinton presidency, his efforts to reverse the tide toward equality were stymied by the change to a progressive presidential administration at the White House. But with the election of George W. Bush in 2000, the scenario was set for a renewal of the old alliance, albeit this time against a different foe. This uneasy marriage has bonded fundamentalist Protestantism and conservative Catholicism in opposition to their new common enemy: feminism.

One value that conservative Catholics and Protestants share in common is a deep distrust of the United Nations. Ever since John Paul II referred to the 1994 Cairo Conference on women as "the work of the devil,"[10] the Catholic Church has mounted a systematic campaign to undermine the work of the United Nations in the advancement of women's equality and reproductive rights and, more recently, the curbing of the worldwide AIDS epidemic. The Vatican did not take much notice of the UN until that body started its major work on advancing women's rights. A latecomer to the world body, the Holy See, as it is known at the UN, was content to use its observer status in a more or less ceremonial way until the Rio de Janeiro Conference of 1988 started to forge links between poverty, environmental degradation, and women's sexual and reproductive rights.

The papacy of John Paul II has seen other moves toward the privatization of morality that has many parallels in the "family values" agenda of the religious right in the United States. This is a tragedy, because it means that, at a time when the globalization of the economy threatens an even greater division of the world between the haves and the have-nots, as well as the continued degradation of the environment, the energies of the churches are narrowly focused on sexual morality. The debate at the UN over the reduction of death by AIDS has shown the obdurate opposition of the Catholic Church to the use of condoms — not just for Catholics, but for everyone. This lobby, consisting of right-wing zealots from hard-line Protestant and Catholic groups who call themselves pro-life, has an agenda that in practice is very much pro-death.

THE ALLIANCE between the Catholic Church and fundamentalist Protestant churches against women's rights and safe sex is a recent phenomenon. Like the hastily cobbled-together alliance between the Vatican and fundamentalist Islamic countries at the UN, it is an alliance born of expediency rather than shared conviction. The primary objective is the silencing of the world movement for the equality of women, which presents the greatest threat to the patriarchal authority rooted in traditional religions. One common theme that unites the right is control of women's sexuality and their bodies.

Jesus and the early Christian communities rejected traditional family values and downplayed the biological role of women as inherently maternal. Christianity was founded not on patriarchal blood or marriage ties, but on an entirely new community of faith, united by a common baptism. In these early Christian communities, people who would not normally have associated together were united in "one faith, one Lord, one baptism" where there was "no longer Jew nor Greek, slave nor free, male nor female" but a oneness derived from Christ. In other words, roles and boundaries of class, nationality, race, and gender were all broken down in the common breaking of the bread of new life. Many at this common table would have been regarded as unclean by reason of their gender, ethnicity. or occupation.[11] Many of the women would have been unmarried, some would have left their husbands, many would not have had children, and some would have been widows or single parents in charge of households. This kind of family was normative in the earliest Christian churches. The kind of "family values" preached by the Christian right today were practiced neither by Jesus nor his followers.

In the cities in which early Christianity flourished, some members of the community would have been unemployed. Today they would be classified as street people, transients, and drifters. But because the early Christians pooled their property, there would have been food, clothing, and money to support these needy members. Private property was held to be so heinously wrong that a couple (Ananias and Sapphira) who secretly held back part of the property they had sold instead of putting all of it into the community fund were struck dead when this was revealed (Acts 5:1–11).

Today's conservative interpretation of family values is far removed from the mores of the Jesus community. Private property is now exalted to the level of a divine right. The religious right's ideal of a patriarchal, heterosexual nuclear family, rejoicing in careful stewardship of its privately owned property, self-satisfied and intolerant of the values and lifestyles of those who are different, is a very far cry from the heterogeneous family of Jesus. The social commitment woven into the economics of early Christian communities has been abandoned. The resurgence of the religious right as a political force in the U.S. Republican Party and in the Alliance Party in Canada has resulted in a sustained attack against state support for welfare, education, and health care. The great exception to state intervention is in the area of women's reproductive rights, which are to be subjected to regulation and public constraint.

The Catholic Church, under the influence of John Paul II, has shown itself remarkably receptive to the siren call of the family values camp. This pontificate has seen a drift toward private morality and away from social morality, except when this impinges on sexuality or women. Rome's obsession with keeping women out of office within the church has led to its repeated assertions that the God-given role of women lies within the private rather than the public sphere. The pope has even issued calls to Catholics to be willing to suffer martyrdom in defense of their beliefs, especially those about sexuality. But most do not see abstaining from sex before marriage or not using a condom in quite the same heroic light as he does.

It was not teachings on contraception, abortion, or homosexuality that got the early Christians martyred, but rather their insistence that since the world and all that was in it belonged to God, there should be no such thing as private property, and all things should be held in common. It was not for teachings on sexuality and privatized morality that Jesus was crucified. It was because his truth about the power of love threatened the truth about the power of authority. It was because the community he created subverted every humanly created division of gender, race, and class that it was such a threat to those whose power rested on dividing and conquering. Although John Paul II has craved martyrdom for himself, it has been bishops such as Oscar Romero of El Salvador, Juan Gerardi Conedera of Guatemala City, and, more recently, the Canadian Jesuit Martin Royackers, all advocates for justice for the poor, who have been the Catholic martyrs of the twentieth and twenty-first centuries.

The credibility of the new lay movements and the family values agenda fails when it is held up to the searing test of love. St. Paul, in the famous passage in 1 Corinthians, places love "above all knowledge, all understanding . . . even the faith to move mountains . . . even giving away all my possessions or handing my body over to be burned at the stake." The evidence of the twentieth century in apartheid, wars, the Holocaust, the poverty of two-thirds of the world, violence against women, ecological devastation and the triumph of competition over compassion, is a powerful testimony that the work of love, of redemption is not yet complete. If we truly believed that the power of the Spirit unleashed on all of us at Pentecost is still operating in each and every one of us, we would go out into the streets and change the world with love.

And yet the patriarchal and hierarchical church has tried to cage the Spirit within the temple. It has claimed to be the only conduit for the Spirit and sought to channel its power within the dry words of dogmas. Authoritarian churches try to shield their adult members from venturing out into the streets and contending with the ambiguities of life. Only a strict adherence to the rules of the church, they allege, will help them to avoid making any mistakes. But this attitude keeps the sacred power of the Spirit in check. It causes people to "play it safe," to avoid putting their lives on the line, and to be ever fearful of the dire consequences of losing control. Jesus did not live a safe life. He was not respectable, neither was he viewed as a nice person by the religious authorities. He posed the kinds of questions they did not want to hear.

This moment in history is a make-or-break time for the institutional Roman Catholic Church and its conservative allies. If they continue to trace a path backward through history into an ideology that owes more to Roman imperial rule than to the Nazarene who was crucified by that empire, they will not and should not survive. Unless the Catholic Church can wean itself from its false apparel of empire, the silken socks and vestments, and the jeweled rings worn by the prince-bishops of the church, then it will become a mausoleum to institutional hubris. At the heart of the Vatican's message lies a refusal to recognize God at work in the modern world. Their version of truth is hostile to the historical experience of the twentieth century and the individual and personal experience of most of humanity.

There is undoubtedly a profound crisis in the world today in reaction to postmodernism. The present moment is uncertain and volatile. The violent backlash of the old world order of domination threatens to overwhelm the new emerging consciousness of connectedness.

Today's supporters of the traditional values of thousands of years of patriarchy, which have led to poverty, sexism, racism, economic dependence, and environmental degradation, have learned to dress up in sheep's clothing and market themselves as merchants of inclusivity and concern. The Vatican's spokespeople speak in glowing terms of the Catholic Church's commitment to its "new feminism" but in practice forbid even the discussion of women priests. The pope exhorts bishops to embrace a life of poverty, but censures leaders such as Bishop Jacques Gaillot of Evreux or Cardinal Evaristo Arns of São Paulo who have taken concrete steps to make the marginalized the center of their concern. The struggle to deconstruct this strategy of deceit and the connection of the churches to the political and religious agenda of the right is a necessary step toward the emergence of the new world order. The compassionate face of God, veiled for too long, is emerging from beneath the *burka* of power and domination. The chapters that follow are intended as a contribution to the struggle to take back the truth of these times.

The Deconstruction of Divinity

Twenty-five years ago I embarked on an intensive period of prayer and conversion of life known as the Spiritual Exercises of St. Ignatius Loyola. This classic program of Catholic spirituality dates from the sixteenth century, when Ignatius Loyola, the founder of the Society of Jesus, began to instruct the lay women who were his earliest followers and to develop a path for them to mystical union with God. Ignatius's efforts initially earned him the censure of the Spanish Inquisition, largely due to the fact that he had chosen to work with women rather than men. He survived the Inquisition and eventually became one of the great reformers of the Catholic Church. He developed the Spiritual Exercises as the formative tool of Jesuit spirituality, and this discipline of prayer has stood the test of time and continues to provide a route for many Christians toward the formation of an adult relationship with God.

The pattern of prayer laid out in the Exercises takes nine months to complete. The version adapted for lay life requires a one-hour daily meditation and review of conscience, frequent journaling, and a weekly meeting with a trained spiritual guide. In the latter part of the cycle of prayer, the retreatant meditates on the passion of Christ. When I was following the Exercises, one week of this section on the passion happened to coincide with Holy Week, so I decided to spend a week at the Jesuit retreat center in Guelph, Ontario, in order to enter more intensively into the experience.

The great insight of the method of contemplation taught by Ignatius is that the retreatant learns to enter into the gospel story. Rather than simply observing the events of the gospel from a distance of time and space, the person who is meditating enters imaginatively into the scene and participates in the action. This permits a free rein for the movement of the Spirit to push the boundaries of spiritual imagination, to venture beyond the text, and to allow the gospel to speak creatively and directly to the circumstances of one's own life.

This takes hard work (it's not called "The Spiritual Exercises" for nothing!) and a great deal of trust in God in order to release any constraints that might restrict God's action. The process involves a step forward into an unknown realm and a letting go of all previous ideas about what is right or wrong in prayer. If the retreatant continues to be open to the Spirit, obstacles to union with God, often long buried in the unconscious, will come to the surface. As these are confronted and surrendered, the retreatant can respond to the loving touch of God.

As I accompanied Christ in prayer through his passion and death that Holy Week, after contemplating the judgment of Jesus by Pilate I was meditating on the scene where he is humiliated, spat upon, and beaten by Roman soldiers. All of a sudden, aghast at what was happening to me but unable to stop myself, I found myself propelled from a spot where I had been sitting in Pilate's courtyard right into the line of soldiers taking their turn to mock Jesus. I realized that I was bent on joining in the humiliation of Christ. The sensation was so strong I physically felt the spittle rise into my mouth as I prepared to launch it at Jesus' face. Then I bolted from the line of soldiers before I got close enough to carry out this intention. At that point, deeply shaken, I stopped the contemplation. My immediate reaction was one of dread as to what I would do next. Would I end up hammering a nail into the hand of Jesus? I wanted to run away from the retreat center and abandon the Spiritual Exercises altogether.

I had come within a hair's breadth of spitting into the face of Jesus. As I reflected further, I sensed that, much as I might like to deny it, I had sometimes metaphorically spat into the face of Jesus as revealed in other people. Despite my intention to follow closely the way of discipleship, left to my own devices I was quite capable of abandoning it. Later I remembered the wisdom of the mystics who have told us that everything we do in prayer and life is the result of the love and the grace of God, not of our own efforts to earn God's favor. God's favor is freely and richly bestowed as a gift, without any strings attached.

Later that evening, after talking over the experience with my Jesuit guide, I decided to continue the Exercises. However, much chastened by this incident, I felt reluctant to approach Jesus closely again as the drama of his trial continued to unfold before me. Like Peter, I lurked in the shadows. But all at once I felt conscious of another presence at my side that I recognized intuitively as that of God the Father. Grasping my hand in his, the Father drew me forward to the front

of the crowd that was walking with Jesus to Calvary. We saw Jesus
stumble and fall under the cross, unable to get up again. I heard a
deep groan from the depths of my companion's soul. His grip on my
hand loosened and I saw him step forward and then kneel down in
the dust to look into the face of his son. Jesus opened his eyes to see
his Father bending tenderly over him. "I can't go on," I heard Jesus
say. "Come, get up, I will help you," was the response. The Father
put his arms around the waist of Jesus, steadied him as he got up,
and heaved the broad beam of the cross onto both their shoulders.
Together they carried the cross for the rest of the way.

Through this insight in prayer, I realized that God had entered
into the vulnerability and weakness of Jesus, not just as the Incar-
nate God, Jesus, but as the Almighty One, transcendent, and Creator
of heaven and earth. God had abandoned his throne. The power of
the Almighty one, the Creator, the All-Powerful, was revealed in overwhelming compassion. I had hitherto never thought of God the Father
as compassionate or close, let alone vulnerable. Merciful perhaps, but
never weak, and always serenely regal.

As a result of unpacking the layers of significance in this mystical/
intuitive experience I came to see that God in Jesus chooses to work
not through domination but through vulnerability. God is not a *deus
ex machina*. Furthermore, God did not inflict the cross on his Son
as some sort of sadistic punishment for the sins of the human race.
God was not, as some varieties of Christian tradition have taught,
weighing the options on whether or not to destroy the world and
then calculating that only the death of his son would be retribution
enough to compensate for the world's evil. Calvary did not take place
because God's wrath and need for satisfaction was aroused. I could
never again experience God as demanding the sacrifice of Jesus as
atonement for sin. Nor could I view God the Father as detached from
the world, looking down from heaven while Jesus went through the
cycle of his life, waiting all the while until he had suffered enough
to pay back the debt to God for humanity's sins. God resisted the
death of His son as much as Jesus did. God did not preordain or
even sanction the crucifixion as the means of our redemption.

The next day, after contemplating the crucifixion itself, I sat in
deep and wordless grief at a place on the edge of the world, a place
that was in time but not of it. I was in the real presence of God as
Mother as well as Father. I sat cradled in the vast lap of God, the
arms of God fastened around me. I noticed there were wounds on

the large, comforting hands of God. The sun was setting in a fiery glow against a rounded hill, and in the distance, outlined against the setting sun, were three empty crosses on its summit. There was complete silence and unutterable sorrow. The grief of God would not be easily assuaged.

I do not claim any universal significance for the individual insights I have been graced with in prayer. But at a deep level, beyond words or rational analysis, I came to know that the God whom I named as Almighty Father at the time could not have been an impassive spectator at the passion. Beyond all confines of time or place, God is present and God weeps every time the innocent suffer. With the help of my spiritual director, it gradually became clear to me that I was experiencing the deconstruction of the God of patriarchy. I was being led into a feminization of God. Divine Wisdom was teaching me in a very direct way to abandon the stern, angry, and vindictive image of God the Father that had been inculcated in me during my childhood, and look instead into a compassionate, vulnerable, and suffering face of God. My urge to spit on the face of Jesus was part of my viscerally negative reaction to my receiving this insight into God's helplessness.

At that time in my life's journey (this was in the early 1980s), I had adapted well to the patriarchal world and had developed a tendency, rather like Margaret Thatcher, who despised the compassion of the "wets" in her conservative caucus, to look down on any demonstration of weakness in the workplace. I was working in a demanding position as principal of a newly created alternative school, and I was on an upwardly mobile career path. As one of only a handful of women then in positions of senior responsibility at the school board, I was fearful of failure and of showing any hint of vulnerability. Any show of weakness on the part of the few women in leadership positions would have been seized on by some as an excuse for alleging that women were not fit to handle the pressures of senior administration. Hence my negative reaction to the helplessness of Jesus. Women who had achieved senior management-level positions within organizations had done so largely at the price of conforming to the boundaries imposed by the corporate culture of the time.

JESUS' LIFE, DEATH, AND RESURRECTION broke through the boundaries imposed by the religious culture of his time. The compassion and vulnerability of God that Jesus preached was not well received. The power of the truth that Jesus lived lay not in a desire for domination,

but in an invitation to live and celebrate "the good news to the poor."
God's liberating energy was shown in Jesus' exorcisms, in his healing
of the sick, and in the celebratory meals at which all were invited to
sit at the table. He tried without success to convert the powerful to
view life as God views it: that human life is best lived in solidarity and
generosity. The powerful in religion and state were threatened by this
vision and sought to destroy the community gathered around Jesus
by orchestrating his terrifying public execution. The resurrection was
the sign that they could not silence him or the prophetic message
that he preached. The risen Jesus now lives on in each generation
wherever prophetic voices arise to reclaim this truth.

In the generation or so immediately after Jesus' death and resurrection, it was within the liturgy, especially the liturgy of baptism, that
the community reenacted the meaning of Jesus' life, death, and resurrection. Some of the earliest Christian literature contains fragments
of hymns and prayers from these early adult baptismal ceremonies,
which were then always carried out by full immersion in water.

One of these is contained in the text of St. Paul's letter to the Philippians. Paul probably wrote to the Christian community in the city of
Philippi sometime after 50 c.e., possibly when he was in prison.[1]
Located in Macedonia, Philippi had been a Roman colony since 40
b.c.e. but retained much of the Hellenistic influence of three hundred years of rule by the royal family that had produced Alexander
the Great. Women in Macedonia were more involved in public social
and economic life than their counterparts elsewhere, and the Christian church there continued to honor this tradition. Lydia, who led
one of the earliest house churches (Acts 16) was from Philippi, as was
Phoebe, one of the leaders of the early church. Two other women
leaders, Evodia and Syntyche, are exhorted by Paul to abandon their
rivalry and come to an understanding (Phil. 4:2).

Such was the setting for one of Paul's warmest and most affection-
ate letters. Because of the negative comments about women attributed
to Paul in the Letter to Timothy (which in fact was probably written
by another author after his death), Paul has gained a reputation as a
misogynist. In practice, however, he seems to have had no problem
in working alongside women in ministry, and he encouraged them to
assume leadership in the communities he created. But like men of his
time, and many of our own age, he could be ambivalent about the
nature and role of women.

The Letter to the Philippians contains a section that may have formed part of the early service of baptism. The hymn-like cadence of this section was likely a compilation of the work of several prophets, of whom there were many, both male and female, in the early church.[2] These are the words that would have greeted the candidates about to immerse themselves in the baptismal waters of life, death, and resurrection in and through Jesus: "Christ Jesus always had equality with God but he did not think to try to grasp at divinity by domination or violence. Instead, he freely gave up what he had, took on the nature of a slave, and became human. He walked the path of obedience all the way to death, death on the cross. For this, God exalted him and gave him a name greater than any other name, so that at the name of Jesus all beings in heaven, on earth, and below will fall on their knees and proclaim Jesus Christ as Lord, to the glory of God the Father" (Phil. 2:1–11).

Jesus, Paul states, did not grasp or personify divinity by domination or violence. This is a key insight into the radical deconstruction of divinity that is represented by the life, death, and resurrection of the God who was in Jesus Christ. Within the terms of postmodern analysis, Jesus would be said to have experienced and taught a "positional disconnectedness" about God. So all previous certainties about God were called into question by the advent of Jesus. And both Caiaphas, who advocated a religious orthodoxy based on a mediation of the power of God through the Temple and its priests, and Pilate, who demanded that religion serve the interests of the empire, conspired to eliminate the threat to their hegemony that was presented by Jesus and his teaching.

Paul's interpretation of the meaning of Jesus' life in the passage from Philippians quoted above is a deconstruction of all forms of divinity represented through power and domination. In and through Christ's passion and resurrection, God critiques all past and future co-options of God's truth as a pretext for power or status. This amounts to a repudiation of all oppressive human dominance that cloaks itself with an aura of divine favor. The intimate movement of Christ's incarnation, the step into this new dance of God and humanity that the prophets of the early Christian communities invited the newly baptized to join, is one that eschews transcendence or power over humanity in favor of partnership and solidarity. This was the message I was learning in the experience of radical discontinuity in my spirituality, and it was one that eventually drew me to challenge the corporate culture of the church and the secular world in which I was deeply immersed.

Humanity in general has found it well nigh impossible to accept a God who is vulnerable. Ever since the fourth century, when Constantine made Christianity into a state religion and tried to fuse the message of Jesus with the dominant power of the imperial state, theologians have tried to reconcile the crucifixion of God with the notion of God's absolute power. Was the cross a necessary part of Jesus' redemptive work of atoning for sin and making satisfaction to a powerful, angry God? That is how many Christian theologians, such as St. Anselm of Canterbury, author of *Cur Deus Homo?* (Why did God become human?), have explained the significance of the crucifixion of Christ. Anselm argued that the human race, through sin, had distanced itself from God. God's anger at humanity's sinfulness could be appeased only by repeated sacrifices offered to atone for sin, but the blood of bulls and goats did not suffice. It was only the sacrificial death of God's own son that paid the debt in full and atoned for humanity's sins. After Calvary, the scales of good and evil (an image much invoked in medieval theological treatises) were once more in balance, and God's wrath was contained. God reined in his desire to destroy the world he had created.

THE HUMAN RACE has just lived through the twentieth century, when violence has taken a terrible toll and the innocent have suffered on a hitherto unimagined scale. If God is all-powerful, many ask, why did God allow this to happen and not intervene to stop it? And how can innocent, unjust suffering and death on such a scale ever be justified as a means of humanity's redemption? There are Christians even today who still preach a perverse answer to this: namely, that all human tragedy is the result of God's deliberate infliction of punishment on humanity for its sins. Even if one were to accept such a theory, for a Christian it amounts to denying the efficacy of Christ's suffering and death.

But the power of the truth at the heart of the life and the teachings of Jesus Christ is that God identifies with the marginalized who are the victims of history. The work of redemption, which is still in process, is accomplished not by violent judgment and the purging of wrongdoers, but by identifying with Jesus in feeding the hungry, clothing the naked, comforting the sorrowful, and giving drink to the thirsty. If the works of love and justice increase, then eventually compassion and solidarity rather than competition and violence will prevail and become the central values of humanity. The cross is the extreme example of the price often paid by those who continue to perform the work of justice and compassion in the face of apathy and hate.[3]

The deconstruction of divinity represented by the life, death, and resurrection of Jesus is consonant with the postmodern deconstruction of history in the West that has placed the victims, history's losers, at the center of historical interpretation, at the expense of the powerful who have hitherto been history's winners. We are now living through an era when every aspect of the past is under scrutiny. The past fifty years have witnessed an intensely controversial deconstruction of power and privilege as this has been exercised historically through the dominance of hereditary systems of class, race, and gender. This dominance has been exercised through political, economic, social, and religious structures and has been deeply embedded in the language, myth, and symbols of Western civilization. The old systems of power and privilege are being deeply challenged by emerging forms of consciousness, many of which are as yet inchoate and have not fully penetrated into established structures. Voices which have previously been unheard in the mainstream "great men's" metanarratives of history are now claiming a voice in the interpretation of that same history, but this time from below. This has sparked conflict at all levels, from the largest international assemblies such as the United Nations, to the intimacy of the bedroom, where personal negotiation of sexual relationships brings issues of power and dominance into the private, intimate realm.

The result of this is that the victims of history now occupy a high moral ground in much of contemporary consciousness. In the West we often sympathize with our ancestors' victims rather than glory in their conquests. This reversal in the public psyche has occurred in large part in reaction to the Nazi Holocaust, which showed how a combination of a twisted interpretation of history and skilful propaganda, embellished by powerful myths and symbols of dominance, can manufacture the consent of a professedly Christian nation for unspeakably inhumane actions. So strong has been the reaction to the violence inflicted on the victims of that dark night of the soul of western Europe that no contemporary or historical event can now be fully assessed until the voices of its victims have been acknowledged and heard. In this context, the relationship of truth to power emerges as a crucial issue. Power and status no longer confer an automatic presumption of integrity.

The only way to interpret today's world, where all previously "certain" truths are now subject to scrutiny, is to go through a process of deconstruction. The illusion that any human person — pope or president — no matter how elevated his or her status, possesses total autonomy of action or can manifest an objectivity of thought that transcends the constraints of time and place is an illusion. It is a legacy of the rationalistic Cartesian, post-Enlightenment world and, in the case of the church, the synthesis of absolute truth with hierarchical power. These past certainties have now proven questionable, and often misleading. No one individual can ever transcend the boundaries of his or her culture, genealogy, and history to the extent that he or she can assume the universal voice of "the human." "It is now necessary to speak of the subject (i.e., the individual human) of reflection as the gospel speaks of the soul. It is necessary to lose it in order to find it."[4]

God, in our time, has stepped away from the throne of heaven and entered into the darkness and discontinuity of our age. Christians are now coming to a new realization of what "The Word made Flesh" means. The leadership of the Catholic Church is currently fiercely resisting the critique and deconstruction of its patriarchal structure because its leadership is unwilling to surrender the throne of their now obsolete certainties. But it is only in losing its life that the church will find it.

This process of discontinuity, an abandonment of what has hitherto been the dominant interpretation of history by its winners, has resulted in what has been called a "surreal confusion" of our age.[5] But now that the weight of historical judgment has shifted in favor of the oppressed, this has caused a discontinuity in the presumption that might is always right. In the fall of 2001, the U.S. and Britain launched a joint attack on Afghanistan in the wake of the September 11 terrorist bombing of the World Trade Center in New York. Some planes dropped bombs, but others followed after them, dropping blankets and food supplies. Bombs and blankets? Was the intent of the exercise to exterminate the terrorists or succor the victims of the bombing? What is the best way to confront terrorism: a global war to eliminate terrorist cells, or a new system of global welfare to eliminate the root causes of terrorism by redistributing wealth in a more equitable manner?

These dilemmas, faced by the nominally Christian nations of the West, are also having an impact on their religious institutions. Two thousand years ago, Jesus was killed as a result of an alliance between the religious and state powers of his world. Ever since Christianity became a state religion, Christians too have killed in the name of God. The fact that the missionary endeavors of Catholic and Protestant churches went hand in hand with the rapacity of Western colonial states is an inescapable fact of more recent history. So what should now be the principal focus of Christian churches? To succor and strengthen the weak, the oppressed, and the marginalized or to judge, punish, and even exterminate unbelievers and sinners? Who speaks for God and God's truth? American fundamentalists Jerry Falwell and Pat Robertson blamed the September 11 attack on feminists, lesbians, and members of the American Civil Liberties Union, all of whom, they said, had made God angry, so that God used the terrorists to punish America. The Islamic terrorists also claimed God was using them to punish America, but Muslim extremists have a different version of America's sins.

The HIV/AIDS crisis has provided another context for the clash of two conflicting religious impulses of our times. Some Christians allege that God is angry about AIDS because it is spread through sex, often same-sex activity, and through drugs, and God is therefore killing off all its victims. AIDS is particularly troublesome for Christian churches because of its association with sexual activity, especially gay sex. For many Christian fundamentalists, and for the Vatican, sexual morality has now become the primary indicator of an individual's fidelity to God. So some Christians insist that AIDS is a sign of the wrath of God toward sinners, and the righteous should leave those guilty of sexual sin to their well-deserved fate. But even if this view of God's response to AIDS was correct, it neglects to take into account that there are also "innocent" victims of AIDS who have not contracted it through illicit sexual activity. And given that one of the causes of the rapid spread of AIDS is the refusal of the Catholic Church to permit the use of condoms, the Catholic Church itself bears responsibility for the death of some of the victims of AIDS.

Others take the view that it is not appropriate for anyone to judge how or why an individual has contracted HIV. It is a situation that should elicit compassion, not judgment. In the light of the gospel story of the woman taken in adultery, no one is in a position to throw stones because all have sinned. The experience of the unconditional love of

God is the most powerful way to move us forward into a state of grace-filled and compassionate living and toward finding a cure for this plague that threatens to wipe out a third of the population in many countries in Sub-Saharan Africa. Christians who see the fate of AIDS sufferers as a well-deserved punishment for sin seem to have forgotten a central truth: the love of God is unconditional and not dependent on our worthiness. Virtuous conduct or goodness is not a precondition for God's love but rather a response to God's favor.

Western civilization came into being as a result of violence and is still being sustained by violence, both military and economic. There is increased questioning of the values of this civilization we have inherited, one that arose as a result of conquest and is maintained by a continued resort to violent domination. The affluence we have inherited is sustained by an economic system that reduces some sectors of the international workforce to virtual slavery and consumes the resources of the earth at unprecedented rates. The violence inflicted on animals in order to feed excessive Western consumption of meat, the removal of diversity in agriculture through genetic engineering, and the increasing environmental cost of the lifestyle of affluent nations have become the focus of various movements of global resistance. Whether or not to continue with a way of life that will eventually threaten the survival of future generations and of the earth itself is probably the most urgent question of our time.

THE POSTMODERN DECONSTRUCTION of history from the vantage point of the victim has not gone unchallenged. It has aroused the ire of those whose power is threatened by voices from the margins. Feminism, environmentalism, anti-poverty movements, and gay rights activism have made considerable inroads into public consciousness. Women's attempts to take back the truth of their experience are now meeting with a backlash from those whose power is most threatened by accepting and implementing the equality of women in all spheres of life. The 1990s witnessed a backlash against the postmodern deconstruction of class and gender privilege. Then and now, in the early years of this new millennium, the gains made by women during the Second Wave of the feminist movement in the 1970s and 1980s have been under sustained attack.[6] Women have had to fight simply to stand their ground and preserve the gains made earlier.

In democratic countries that at least pay lip service to the value of equality, some of the traditional power brokers of society have resisted these gains, not by mounting a frontal attack on the newly emerging consciousness, but by a resort to ridicule and sarcasm. The label "politically correct" has come into usage in an effort to discredit feminism or environmentalism or other movements for equity and rob them of their impact. "Jock" talk-radio shows lament the extinction of the world of "real men." Slipshod definitions of views that dissent from the status quo as reflecting only "special interest groups" caricature their proponents as pitiable whiners. The interests of the dominant group are always presented as universal, and the truths and values sanctioned by the status quo as benevolent and universally applicable. But groups that so ingenuously benefit from the power conferred upon them are never subjected to scrutiny.

The latest political resurgence of the right has coincided with a reemergence of right-wing religious movements. The restorationist papacy of Pope John Paul II, the revival of the evangelical Christian right in the United States, and the rise of fundamentalist Islamic movements in the Arab world mark a historical convergence that threatens to undermine the gains made by formerly marginalized groups as the secular world has moved in the direction of pluralism and democracy. With the inauguration of George W. Bush in January 2001, there has been a marriage of social conservatives in church and state. This has left many people with a sinking feeling that history is about to repeat itself. The Christian religion has a long history of acting as a complicit ally of nations and states that have colonized and forcibly converted what is now the poor two-thirds of the world and subjected women, homosexuals, blacks, and indigenous peoples to second-class status and even to slavery.

The present moment in history is therefore fraught with both danger and opportunity, in religion no less than in other spheres. To take back the truth from power and claim it and sustain it requires courage and creativity. It is through the influence of various theologies of feminism and liberation that the patriarchal religions in the West could be on the verge of a deep breakthrough in cosmic consciousness into a realization of the feminine in God. That change requires of humanity that people become immersed in love — lover of ourselves and lover for all the rest of creation. This means that we will have to detoxify ourselves of an addiction to a God who purportedly speaks the truths of power. To realize the truth of the gospel is to realize that God desires the harm of no creature on earth and suffers when hurt is inflicted in any way.

The truth manifested in the life, death, and resurrection of Jesus is that God prefers to suffer violence rather than to sponsor it. Jesus Christ preached that truth with authenticity because he also lived in and through that truth. The greatest "preachers" of the twentieth century, Mahatma Gandhi and Martin Luther King, also lived this truth. Both taught that at the heart of God's truth is love — a love that burns for the downtrodden and longs for the day when they will be lifted up and realize their full worth within the circle of humanity. The truth that these witnesses lived is full of power: true, authentic power. Given the fragility of this reality and the extent of the present backlash directed against it, it is important for all who struggle to continue to live the values of Jesus, Gandhi, and King to exercise vigilance, and to challenge the religious power plays that are attempting to do an end run on inclusiveness and tolerance.

As a Catholic, I find great cause for concern in the direction taken by the Catholic Church in the past twenty-five years. There has been a return to a conspicuous reconfiguration and reassertion of centralized papal monarchy within the church. Long ago, out of the ashes of the church's close association with the imperial ethos of ancient Rome, was constructed an imperial form of Christianity where Christ reigned in the likeness of an emperor — the Dominator, Judge, Kyrios, and Lord of history. The church would become the visible incarnation of Christ's power on earth, modeled after the kyriarchal-hierarchical structure of heaven.[7] For centuries afterward, the Catholic Church sought to control the direction of history by power and influence rather than by persuasion. Popes and bishops resorted to war, executions, torture, inquisition, silencings, and excommunication with the truth often sacrificed at the altar of power.

This idea of the necessity for sacrificial violence in the service of truth is one of the defining constructs at the heart of patriarchal culture.[8] It is seductive and deep-rooted, and it has recently been resurrected in the Catholic Church. It is precisely this myth of sacrificial violence, though, that was challenged and overthrown in the passion and death of Jesus. But the concrete realization of Jesus' radical challenge to the truths manufactured and enforced by power has proven to be elusive, because the myth of sacrificial violence is embedded in many of the religious texts of the Judeo-Christian tradition.

It is an inescapable fact that the Bible often sanctions violence as a way of establishing the superiority of the truth of the one God. Israel's conquest of the Promised Land was effected at the point of the sword. The judges and later the kings led armies into battle in the name of the Lord. The psalmist calls out for the extirpation of God's enemies. This culture of religiously sanctioned violence characterizes much of the scriptural story, and it is a recourse to what the feminist scriptural scholar Phyllis Trible named "texts of terror" that forms the core of the fundamentalist Christian message of today.[9]

The idea of the wrath of the one true God held in readiness to be unleashed against sinners and unbelievers has become one of the central pillars of Protestant fundamentalism. Fundamentalists also hold to the atonement/satisfaction theory of redemption according to which God's wrath was finally appeased by the substitution of the life of His Son offered as a sacrifice for the sins of humanity. They use selective reading and literal interpretation of certain texts in the Bible to support a rigid and punitive set of theological views. (A more detailed examination of the fundamentalist movement, its views, and its relationship to reactionary groups within the Catholic Church will be undertaken in chapter 4.) The eruption of the Christian right onto the U.S. political scene in the 1970s, with its platform of social conservatism and its sanctioning of competitive capitalist values, has placed these "truths" at the service of the power of the Republican Party.

THE POLITICAL IMPACT of the ideology of the religious right and its appropriation of the label "Christian" for hate-filled propaganda and exclusionary views has caused many, especially feminists, to come to the conclusion that the Bible is beyond redemption. The biblical God and the patriarchal aspects of the Christian religions that he appears to sanction seem to be intrinsically violent and misogynist. The fact that fundamentalists today pick out the most extreme passages from the Bible to justify the infliction of hatred and violence on individuals or groups reinforces this impression. The betrayal, rape, and dismemberment of the unnamed concubine from Bethlehem (Judg. 19:1–30), the sacrifice of Jephthah's daughter in fulfillment of his vow (Judg. 4:29), and the rape of Tamar by her brother Amnon (2 Sam. 13:1–22) are examples of texts that one would wish could be erased from the Bible.

The revelation of God is neither static nor linear, however, but evolutionary. God, and God's divine Wisdom, were active in the world and in human consciousness long before the Bible and are still at work today outside the confines of biblical religions. The Bible is not the only vehicle for the revelation of God. Humanity, made in the image of God, also has its own grace-filled insights. One of the insights of postmodern philosophy is that every text has a context, and the context of the author has influenced the text. The contemporary experience of democracy and of the equality of women and men has resulted in a more critical scrutiny of biblical texts. Biblical studies, archaeology, and literary criticism have shed light on the varied context reflected in the diverse authorship of the Bible and the evolution of God's revelation within the biblical text. In the light of human experience and critical evaluation, certain passages of the Bible are now viewed as counter-revelatory of God's love. Human sacrifice, for example, can never be justified. Rape is a crime of violence, not a pursuit of male honor. The commandment to "honor thy father and mother" is the wrong advice for abused children. The injunction of the Letter to the Ephesians to wives to be subject to their husbands does not sanction wife-beating or require married women to submit to unlimited sexual demands on the part of their husbands.

The Bible also contains another set of themes that call into question the sacralization of violence. It reveals a God who abominates sacrifice, renounces force, and shows forth the truth of compassion. As early as the myth of Cain and Abel, which is recounted in the fourth chapter of Genesis, God categorically rejects violence. The blood of the murdered Abel, the peaceful cultivator of the land, cries out to God from the earth that it has besmirched. Cain goes forth not as a founding father but as a branded murderer. The biblical renunciation of sacrificial violence keeps reappearing, albeit at times embedded within a triumphalism that continues to celebrate conquest and oppression.

Even the story of Abraham and Isaac, so ambiguous in its portrayal of a God who appears to test the limits of human fidelity in the cruelest possible way, ultimately rejects the perpetration of violence. The release of Abraham from this blood sacrifice eventually led to a whole new trajectory in Israel away from sacrifice, animal and human, altogether. On this occasion, God sends a ram, and Isaac is spared. This story features prominently in medieval Christian atonement theology, in which Isaac, the only child of Abraham and Sara, is viewed as a symbol of Christ. The sacrifice of God's only son is an atoning action that averts the wrath of God against sinners. In some liturgical texts, Christ is compared both to Isaac the only son, and to the ram substituted for Isaac.

But Christ himself did not identify his mission with any of these texts of sacrifice. It was neither the sacrificial ram nor the Passover lamb that he chose as the sacrament of his continuing presence with us, but rather bread and wine. It was not a sacrifice to appease God's wrath that was emphasized at Jesus' table, but a joyful sharing of community, using the simple fruits of the earth. It is not the blood of the lamb or the blood of Christ, now so prominent in right-wing evangelical theology, which is used as the primary symbol of Christian initiation, but water, the water of baptism. Jesus' own life and teaching are not rooted in a belief in the wrath of God, but in the other theme that also emerges in the Bible — that of the God of Israel who is the champion of the weak, the outcast, and the victim. This God is moved by suffering. This God admits to feeling pain, sorrow, and desire.

Glimpses into this vulnerability of God are found in other texts of the Hebrew scriptures. There is one telling incident recorded in the first book of Kings. The prophet Elijah, meditating in the cave on Sinai where he had spent the night, was allowed to catch a glimpse of God passing by (1 Kings 19:9–14). God was not in the fierce wind that came and split the rocks of the mountain, nor in the earthquake and the fire which followed. After the fire, God came in the silence and whispered to the prophet in a still, small voice. Today there is again a yearning to catch a glimpse of this gentle God who walks often unseen through the highways and byways of the world and whose footsteps only the mystic can hear. In increasing numbers, people are abandoning institutional Christianity to search for God outside the churches: in nature, in Elijah's cave.

The biblical texts manifest a tension between Israel's dependence on the power of sacred violence and domination, and its moral and theological ambivalence about the system of war and the destruction of human life to which this has led. This same tension is being played out today. There is a division now within Christianity that cuts across denominational lines. It is between those who believe in religion as dominance and those who believe in religion as liberation. Those who believe the God who works through power and domination, be they Jew, Christian, or Muslim, also hold that the state, through its laws and law enforcement, should be a vehicle of enforcing their particular set of beliefs. Religion has been used in recent years in nations such as the United States, Israel, and Afghanistan as a means of strengthening ethnic or national identity. Over and against this, though, is a newly emerging global consciousness of religion as pluralistic and nonviolent, operating by persuasion and example rather than by coercion. Resolution of the tension between these two religious worldviews is essential to the realization of peaceful co-existence in the twenty-first century.

Ultimately, the God of the Bible rejects violence of any kind. This comes out most clearly in the writings of the prophets and in the wisdom literature of the Jewish scriptures. The prophets envisage a world made intelligible not by divine wrath but by divine empathy. In the writings of Amos, prophet of the Northern Kingdom of Israel, God states: "I hate and despise your feasts, I take no pleasure in your solemn festivals. When you offer me holocausts I reject your solemn oblations and refuse to look at your sacrifices of fattened cattle. Let me have no more of the din of your chanting, no more of your strumming on harps. But let your justice flow like water and integrity like an unfailing stream" (Amos 5:21–24).

In the book of the prophet Isaiah there is a later section attributed to a writer who has now become known as Deutero, or Second, Isaiah. This middle section outlines a vision of a prophetic figure who has come to be known as the Servant of God. The Suffering Servant poems portray a person formed by God in the womb and called to establish justice on the earth. Gentleness, courage, and hope characterize the life of the Servant of God, even though he is prepared to suffer insult and humiliation in the pursuit of the mission. Finally, the servant is arrested, beaten, and killed by the mob, but his death is seen as a "sacrifice of forgiveness" that restores Israel to God's favor. In the Book of Acts, the apostle Philip chooses this text as a vehicle for explaining the death of Jesus to an Ethiopian he met on the road from Jerusalem to Gaza (Acts 8:26–40). In so doing, he assures posterity that this text will hold a key place in the Christian understanding of the meaning of Jesus' crucifixion. But there remains an inescapable ambiguity in this text because it portrays the victim of violence as the agent of God's self-revelation, at the same time that it declares that God appears to be pleased with the innocent suffering of the victim of violence.

In an earlier text of the Bible, the Book of Wisdom, the portrait of God is painted with an exquisite gentleness. Divine Wisdom, or "Sophia" in Greek, appears as a late development of revelation in the Hebrew scriptures. It reflects the influence of Hellenistic thought which the people of Israel encountered in the period after their exile from Jerusalem scattered them throughout the Near Eastern world.

There they were exposed to new religious currents of thought. The sacrificial observances, which had been the central point of religious practices centered on the Temple in Jerusalem, could no longer be the focus of their worship.

The divine feminine figure of Sophia has reappeared like a "silver vein" in the dark face of patriarchal texts of scripture that women are currently mining.[10] Divine Wisdom is at once the architect of the world who shares the throne of God and the practical and compassionate woman who provides for her cosmic household and goes searching in the streets for people to invite to her table. She is intelligent and holy. The power and radiant beauty of her truth is subtle and mystical. Her power lies in persuasion and attraction, not in domination. Such was the Divine Wisdom who dwelt within Jesus, whom Paul refers to as the "Sophia" of God (1 Cor. 1:30).

When God, in Jesus, chose to become human, it was also with an exquisite gentleness. God, in Jesus, chose not to dominate the human race, but to demonstrate a radically new way of being strong that comes through vulnerability. Jesus did not deliberately seek out martyrdom by a violent death. There is a crucial difference between actively seeking death and pursuing one's ideals even when these lead to a situation where death is a possible outcome. We have been so inured to hearing the death and resurrection stories of the gospel in quick succession that it is now impossible to break out of idealizing Christ's death, because we know it was going to be followed by resurrection. Jesus may have been surprised by his arrest. To be sure, he had made enemies. He had inveighed against the religious elites who had domesticated the wild desert truth of Yahweh's people into a series of ritual regulations over which they had absolute control. As a Galilean of questionable or even illegitimate birth, Jesus would have been ostracized by the "pure" class of priests in Jerusalem. "From the beginning of his life Jesus negotiated the treacherous terrain between belonging to the people of God and ostracism in his own community."[11]

The meals around which Jesus built so much of his ministry were intended to replace the sacrificial offerings of the temple priests. While they performed these ritual actions to appease God and purify the community, Jesus' meals gathered all without discrimination as a sign that God's reign was already present. Those who recognized God as love are gathered into the earthly banquet where this abundant love is shared. The power of the truth that Jesus lived is that this God is present wherever bread is broken and wine is poured out. It is a dangerous truth. It can create a community of equals that breaks through the boundaries of class, creed, or gender. This is a threat to those who believe that power is bestowed from above and diffused on earth through hierarchical structures. God's power at work in Jesus is shown through alignment with the suffering of the victim rather than through controlling the world by collaborating with the powerful. His contemporaries rejected this and it is still rejected by Christians today. The gospels witness to the difficulty that the disciples experienced in understanding this upside-down theology. They wanted Jesus to demonstrate his power to show the truth of his preaching. Invoking the raw power of God was one of the temptations that Satan, the originator of the great lie of truth at the service of power, placed before Jesus in the temptations in the desert. "Throw yourself down from the height and surely your God will protect you and let me help you take over all the kingdoms of the world" (Matt. 4:8).

The crucifixion of Jesus demystifies this demonic use of violent power. Evil cannot penetrate or co-opt such astounding divine vulnerability. Christ's crucifixion inaugurates a new epoch where any kind of violence used in the service of religion will come to be viewed as contrary to God's design. This is a long way still from realization. The deconstruction of history in favor of its victims that is happening in the present age is part of this process of redemption begun by Christ. The myth of divine violence in the service of righteousness has dogged Christian history. The demystifying of violence is an arduous task. "The victim has the last word in the Bible, and we are influenced by this even though we do not want to pay the Bible the homage it deserves."[12]

By arousing empathy for victims, the gospel disrupts the kind of peace and social consensus that primitive religions and cultures were once able to achieve at the expense of the victims of sacrificial violence, whether this was symbolic or actual.[13] The crucifixion marks a sharp discontinuity with all previous religious systems based on power. The democratic tradition of the Western world, which protects the human rights of all and attempts at least to include all in the political and decision-making process, is inherited partly from the Christian vision of universal inclusion and justice, especially for the most marginalized. Sadly, it is within the Christian churches themselves that the struggle for equality and inclusiveness has often met with the most intractable opposition.

THERE IS, HOWEVER, a note of caution that must be introduced into this articulation of the centrality of victims within the design of God. Feminists have subjected the biblical revelation of a God who is vulnerable and who identifies with the victim to critical examination by a hermeneutic of suspicion. Why? Because women in patriarchal Christian societies have been made to assume the role of sacrificial victims. A woman's duty as wife and mother has been to give her life in the service of her husband and children. This pattern of domestic submission has been invested with the religious sanction that it constitutes women's primary means of achieving salvation. Women's biological gift of birthing has been enlarged into an exclusive role as the nurturers of the human race, as the tamers of the brute nature of men, and as the sacrificial appeasers of the violence inherent in patriarchal culture. When women suffer abuse, violence, death even, at the hands of a partner, they have been taught to endure this for the sake of the preservation of the family and of society.

Women have been socialized for so long with an ethic of unselfish care for the welfare of others that they have learned not to care for themselves. They are expected to be inured to suffering because this is a result of their dedication to the welfare of others. Women in the Christian community have been told to identify with the silence of Mary, the mother of Jesus, as well as with the suffering of Jesus on the cross. If they "offer up" the trials and tribulations of their inferior status, says this theology, their suffering will make them more identical to Christ. Their passive endurance is redemptive and will save their husband, their nation, and their world. Women abused by their husbands have been counseled by priests in confession to return to their marriage and offer up their sufferings to God to effect a change of heart in their man. A holy woman can redeem the raw lust of male sexual urges. The idea that suffering is redemptive and that the meek suffering of women will save the world is still very much part of papal discourses on women. So unless women are being self-sacrificing, the implication is, they are not good women and the violence that may be inflicted on them to bring them into line is deserved. Not only do these attitudes perpetuate the idea of a masochistic God and encourage passivity in women, but they also prevent women from taking the necessary steps to disengage themselves from dangerous situations.

Hence the idea that the victim occupies the center of history is an appealing but also potentially dangerous one for women. If one simply moves the victim to the center of concern in order to elicit compassion but nothing is done to confront the systemic cause of the violence against victims, then the role of passive victim becomes implicitly sacralized. The systemic, violent dominance of oppressors that has produced the situation will remain unchallenged and intact. Thus violence against women becomes remythologized and the mimetic cycle of violence continues. The redemption of the evildoer comes at the price of the victims' suffering.

The suffering, and even the sacrifice, of the victim of social oppression may relieve the symptoms of the society's addiction to competition and violence, but it will not ipso facto change the system. To focus on the victimization of women, to even exalt the status of the victim to one of central concern without confronting the patriarchal structures of church and society which have produced this situation is like taking an aspirin to cure a terminal disease. In the short term, there will be a relief from suffering. In the long term it is justice — not merely charity — that is required.

In more modern times and especially since the industrial revolution, the factory system imposed long hours and degrading conditions of work for men. The passive role of women as the guardians of hearth and home has been romanticized, especially in papal writings. Because women were excluded from paid work, they became the repositories of qualities such as nurturing, compassion, and vulnerability, which were banished from the workplace because of the demands of the competitive, capitalist economy. This role placed women on a pedestal of goodness and innocence, above the sweaty, brutish conditions men endured in their daily labor. The "good woman's" role was to preserve her home as a sanctuary where children could be raised in safety and men could come back for repose at the end of the day. Women were expected to submerge any desire for their own autonomy or self-realization and to accept passively whatever suffering came their way because this was part of the sublime role God created for them when He gave them the biological means of becoming mothers. Motherhood can also be viewed as a substitute for martyrdom. This exaltation of motherhood and the domestic domain still features in church writings on women, which only reluctantly acknowledge that women now have the opportunity to move out of the domestic realm and into the public realm of work.

How can women find a way out of the trap of victimization? Has the atonement theology so penetrated the core of the thinking of the churches that, as many women now contend, Christianity is irredeemable and will never provide an equal and honorable place for women within its structures? To accept a vulnerable God as a model might mean simply confirming the stereotypes forced on women for so long by church and society. The key to release from this conundrum lies in reexamining the role of Jesus. The vulnerability of God in Jesus is not passive; neither is it imposed from outside. It results from his freely chosen and risky identification with the marginalized. This is the role model of Christian discipleship that applies to both men and women and was lived by both genders in early Christian communities.

Another solution is to replace the theology of sacrifice and atonement that has permeated so much of Christian spirituality with the theology of struggle and liberation. In the life of Jesus, God brings forth life not because of Jesus' suffering but in spite of it. Right up to the end, Jesus resisted nonviolently the forces that threatened to overwhelm him. Jesus died not because a bloodthirsty God demanded that the sins of humanity be washed clean through the blood sacrifice of the lamb but because Jesus refused to change course from the radical challenge he had issued to unjust relationships in the family and in religious institutions. God does not demand suffering as the sine qua non for redemption. If it comes, as it inevitably will when people challenge the truths of the powers with the power of truth, then the resurrection of Jesus demonstrates that God can work to lead beyond suffering to new life.

Jesus overturned the idea of a sacrifice as atonement and sacrificial meals as pleasing to God by instituting meals with outcasts. This is the sacrifice — the circumcision of the heart that the prophet Jeremiah referred to — which Jesus showed was the one pleasing to God. His meals with prostitutes, street people, tax collectors, and others labeled by the pious as sinners relativized all the cultural and religious restrictions around who was pure or impure and who could therefore partake or be excluded from the table of God. The table fellowship with outcasts was the most conspicuous feature of Jesus' ministry. With apologies to Marshall MacLuhan, the meal was the message. "Jesus' burning passion was to free those he encountered from the grip of religious mystification and scandalous delusion whose effects were to harden the human heart and turn people into accomplices of cruelty and lovelessness."[14]

The Christian liturgical year opens with the season of Advent, which spans four weeks of preparation for the feast of Christmas. The readings of Advent combine the prophetic longing and hope for the coming of God in the Hebrew scriptures with gospel texts that illustrate how Jesus revealed the presence of God in the flesh. One of the recurring themes of the readings is the banquet table of God. The vision of the prophet Isaiah — that "the Lord will make for all peoples a feast of rich food, of well-aged wines.... God will wipe away the tears from all faces and will take away humiliation from all people" (Isa. 25:6–10) — is combined with a text from Matthew's Gospel. "Great crowds came to Jesus," he writes, "bringing with them the lame, the maimed, the blind, the mute, and many others. They placed them at his feet and he cured them." After the healing, Jesus turned to assuage the hunger. "I have compassion on the crowd," he said, "because they have been with me now for three days with nothing to eat: and I don't want to send them away hungry because they might faint on the way home" (Matt. 14:13–21). Then he gathered seven loaves and four fishes and shared these among the crowd.

This meal that Jesus shared was about healing hurt and relieving hunger. Bread is broken and shared among broken people as a sign that the greatest desire in the heart of God is to "wipe the tears away from all faces and take away the humiliation from all people." The miracle that took place with the sharing of the loaves and fishes was also a miracle about breaking down religious prejudice. Matthew's Gospel was written with Jewish readers in mind. Observant Jews would have brought kosher food with them to this meeting with Jesus to avoid transgressing dietary laws. The story implies that food was shared among clean and unclean alike, symbolizing the inclusiveness of God's banquet table. This was a "hands on" lesson for them about life in the new "kindom"[15] as opposed to "kingdom" of God, which will be a life with an open heart that transcends all religious and social barriers.

But the contagious power of violence in the service of "truth" still exercises its fascination within the church today. One of the most telling acts in the latter days of the papacy of John Paul II has been the return to strict exclusionary laws around the reception of the Eucharist. No Catholic who is divorced and remarried, who is an active homosexual, who has had an abortion, or who is using contraception may approach the communion table. Also, no Catholic lay person may now touch the vessels used by the priest in the Mass, not even to wash them. Only a priest's anointed hands (hands which are also forbidden to caress a woman) are pure enough to handle the sacred plate and cup. These kinds of barriers around the eucharistic banquet table have made churches into places where many people experienced cruelty and lovelessness. How distant all of this is from the festive community meals celebrated by Jesus.

When she refers to Christian discipleship, theologian Elizabeth Johnson says that it has a "paschal character." The Risen Jesus is neither passive victim nor dominating lord, but rather demonstrates the liberating Word and Wisdom of God in solidarity with the poor. After the resurrection, Jesus was recognized only by those who believed in him. The women, whose history and experience of vulnerability attracted them to Christ, are able to see the Risen Christ before the men. Although the disciple John is placed at the foot of the cross in the fourth gospel, he was among those in the upper room who initially doubted the women's testimony of resurrection. For all of them, the sight of Jesus alive provides the hope that the most terrible suffering imposed at the hands of the truth in service to power is not the end of the story. The empty tomb also means that Jesus' resting place could not be made into a shrine where the memory of murder can become a justification for vengeance and for more victims and violence.

The significance of the resurrection is that the historical Jesus of the four gospels does not have the last word on Christianity. Neither is that word locked up within the texts of the gospels. Jesus is still traveling the path of history and goes ahead of us. If we believe his own words, we shall come to do greater things than he did. The Spirit, Jesus said, will accomplish in the remaining epochs of history what was begun at the crucifixion. "The Paraclete," which is one of the names given to the Spirit in the Gospel of John, is the one who defends the accused ones. She (and I use the feminine advisedly because in both the Aramaic and the Hebrew spoken by Jesus the words for "spirit" are feminine) will rise up in the voices of those who uncover the myths of truth at the service of power.

The work of the Spirit in the church and in the world is the reason that Christianity is not irredeemable. All theology is limited by the contextual framework of its age. In other words, it is burdened by the limits of the context within which it is articulated. Christian truth cannot be mediated today through words or images that undermine

its message. The gender-exclusive male language for God and humanity, for example, is one such obstacle for the contemporary reader. It
is one reason that so few people today look to church documents for
enlightenment. But even as theology, liturgy, poetry, and prayer attempt to capture in words our relationship to God, theologian, priest,
poet, or mystic will all at some stage cry out with the phrase of the
medieval mystic Meister Eckhart: "I pray God to rid me of God."
No finite word can ever be the final word about the infinite essence
of God. Each succeeding age must take back God's truth and reclaim
it from the lies that have perverted it in the service of domination.

_____

THREE

The Ambiguous Legacy of John Paul II

In the fall of 1997, a group of eleven men and women knocked on the door of the Vatican and asked to see the pope. They had come bearing hundreds of thousands of signatures from all over the world in support of the reform of the church. They wanted to deliver them in person to the Shepherd of the flock of Christ, who also bears the title of supreme Pastor of the church. They had sent a letter in advance to announce their intentions but had received no acknowledgment of their request for a meeting.

They were halted in their tracks by the crossed lances of the Swiss Guards. When they announced that they had come to Rome from all over the world and had sent a letter to the pope prior to their arrival, a guard was dispatched down the gilded interior hall of the Vatican. The lances remained crossed, barring their entry. A few minutes later the guard returned with a priest in a cassock. The priest peered out over the guards' weapons and nervously requested that one person only come in with the petition. The lances were drawn back to allow Elfriede Harthe, representative of IMWAC (International Movement We Are Church) to pass through. She was swiftly ushered out of sight by the nervous priest, and they met behind one of the pillars in the hallway for a furtive, hurried conversation. She presented the petition to him. That was the last she or anyone else in the delegation heard of it. "I felt," she wrote later, "like a poor widow who had been admitted at the entrance of the king's palace in order to avoid the appearance of condescension but with the clear intention of conveying to her the magnificence of absolute royal power and her own comparative insignificance."

One early spring morning roughly two millennia ago, another group of women set out together before dawn, carrying jars of precious spices and ointments. Mary, the mother of Jesus, was there, along with Mary of Magdala, Salome, Joanna, Mary, the mother of James, and others. They had come to anoint the dead body of Jesus, but when they arrived at the tomb the great stone had been rolled away. Aghast and fearful that they were about to come upon some grisly desecration to Jesus' body, they went into the tomb and found a young man sitting there. "Jesus of Nazareth is not here," he told them. "He has risen to life and has gone on ahead of you to Galilee. Go and tell Peter and the others that he will meet you there."

Consider what happened next in Luke's version. The women ran back to where the apostles were still sleeping, safe inside the locked doors of the Upper Room. The women's importunate knocking roused them, grumbling, from their slumber. The bolts were drawn back and Mary, Joanna, and the others burst in with their news. Shocked and bewildered, the men shook their heads. "You women are obviously hysterical," they said. "You've lost it. Calm down and get your emotions under control. Then we'll see if we can make any sense out of your crazy story." When the men eventually followed the women to the tomb on Easter Sunday, they too found it empty.

Elfriede Harthe has worked in the international women's movement and been a leading spokesperson of the European Church Reform coalition for many years. She described her feelings as she came out of the Vatican as "coming out of a mausoleum into the fresh air." The magnificent interior of the Vatican was hushed and grand, but bereft of signs of life. The palaces of the Vatican still stand in splendor today, memorials erected to celebrate the shadow of papal power in a bygone age. These palaces are carefully guarded against unwelcome intruders.

Pilate set up guards with lances at the tomb, but they could not block Jesus' exit. Jesus moved on, and the tomb is empty. Those who still remain guarding the Vatican mausoleum today are intent on trying to anoint a dead body. Jesus has gone. He has eluded the gilded chains of their past glories, and is out and about on the road. He can never be kept dead and buried in a guarded tomb or chained within a dogmatic formula. That original Easter message, delivered by the women who went running out of the empty rock carved out of the hillside near Calvary, keeps reappearing in unexpected places.

Familiarity, it is said, breeds contempt. Familiarity with Luke's story of the resurrection has bred perhaps not contempt but lethargy in most of us, who have heard this or other versions of the resurrection narrative year after year on Easter Sunday. The potential power of the proclamation of this truth gets domesticated amid the white vestments, glorious flowers, chocolate eggs, and fluffy Easter bunnies. The power of the truth spoken by the women who had stood by the cross and witnessed the resurrection has been trivialized, nowhere more so than within the churches themselves.

The women followers of Jesus, following his own example, challenged the assumptions of their contemporaries on the appropriate role and place for women. Jesus not only tolerated women disciples; he positively encouraged them to assume a place alongside the men, much to the scandal of not only his enemies, but his own family. Jesus never assigned any woman a role based on biology or on her maternal instincts; neither did he give women a separate message from men about what it means to be his follower. The power of this truth that shines through the fleeting but fierce stories in the gospel cannot be buried under the truths of the powers in the Catholic Church despite their refusal to engage with the message that women are announcing to the church. Even though the doors of the Catholic Church remain bolted in fear against them, women are taking back the liberating truth of the gospel and, in the process, opening up new rooms in the household of God.

Jesus' practice presents a stark contrast to the way today's successors of the apostles respond to the Marys, the Joannas, the Elfriedes, who come knocking on their doors.

One of the initiatives of the later part of John Paul II's papacy has been to attempt to domesticate the feminist movement to make it fit within the Catholic Church's construction of so-called "eternal" truths about women. The Vatican seems to have realized that the feminist movement is here to stay, so it has abandoned its initial strategy of combating it head on. Now it is attempting to pare down women's demands for complete equality into a shape that will fit a patriarchal model that holds the line against women priests.

In order to combat women's advance toward equality, so threatening to the status quo within the Catholic Church, John Paul II invented what he calls his "new feminism." In his writings about women — and they have been prolific — he is now attempting to co-opt the language of feminism in order to subvert the substance of its message. The truth that feminism is attempting to articulate is twisted to fit the truth of power. One of the most threatening aspects of feminism for the church's leaders comes from postmodern analysis, where gender is seen as a social and cultural construct rather than an unchanging biological given. This analysis lays bare the systemic sexism on which many policies and practices of the Catholic Church have been constructed.

According to John Paul's "feminism," men and women are equal but their natures are different and their roles complementary. God created masculine and feminine natures separately, each with its own special gifts. Nothing must interfere with the Creator's design as this is interpreted by the pope. The sublime gift of women's nature, he argues, is motherhood. The complementary but different gifts of men's nature have never been set forth in the pope's analysis of womanhood nor in any of his other teaching. Men's nature is accepted as a given. Fatherhood simply makes men more like God and masculinity makes them more like Christ. So the exclusive privilege of Holy Orders, and hence the exclusive right to rule and guide the church, is a role he has declared to be appropriate only for men. Motherhood in the human family, it appears, does not endow women with the appropriate gifts to minister within Mother Church.

In order to perpetuate the exclusion of women from the Catholic priesthood, the Vatican continues to define women's nature as primarily maternal, nurturing, and passive as opposed to men's nature, which is primarily dominant, aggressive, and active. Modern papal teaching reiterates the old dualism that supported the subordination of women but dresses it up in contemporary language. Defenders of John Paul's "new feminism" argue that it is based on an exalted view of the role of women. But however exalted his view of motherhood, church teaching still sees women as primarily the means of their children's and husband's fulfillment, with the implication that women who seek fulfillment in a role outside the home or women who choose to be childless are somehow deficient in femininity.

It is true that men and women are not identical, but the modern world has long since accepted that the biological differences between them are compatible with social equality and vocations to similar social roles.[1] Gender difference need not mean gender dominance. Women's human rights are not gender-specific. They are human rights just as men's are. Feminism does not seek to abrogate the common humanity shared by men and women, or to "masculinize" women, but it does seek to expose, critique, and change the way this common humanity has been structured hierarchically in favor of men. The male celibate view of women that has dominated the theology of the church for two thousand years is not open to these insights. Church leaders cannot envisage a woman as what postmodern philosophy refers to as a "multiple subject" — i.e., a person who can have multiple identities and roles. The clergy clearly envisage men, like themselves for example, in multiple roles and identities both within and outside the church. So while the leadership of the Catholic Church insists that it supports an equal but complementary role for women, their statements about the nature of God and of humanity continue to reflect the projection of their own idealized male human nature.[2]

For this as well as for other reasons, I believe that John Paul II's pontificate will come to be seen by historians as the beginning of the end of authoritarian, hierarchical, and paternalistic thinking in the Catholic Church. The church's attempt to impose its truth by doing violence to the aspirations of women is already viewed by the majority of Catholics as misguided, if not heretical.[3] John Paul II has undoubtedly raised the profile of the Catholic Church on the global scene, and, in an extraordinarily active pursuit of "foreign policy," he has intervened with mixed success in affairs of state all over the world. His papacy has been strong on style but weak on substantive engagement with the world on its own terms and on its own turf. Even though he has traveled more than any other pope in history and preached his truth to the world, he has failed to encounter the real world that is out there on the roads of Galilee and listen to the truth of its experience.

It is time to take the truth back out of the Upper Rooms of the Vatican and out to the streets of the world.

THERE IS LITTLE reciprocal understanding on the part of the church toward the world. Today's Catholic Church, and its recent allies in conservative Protestant churches, preach at the world but do not listen to or receive the wisdom of its experience. The legacy of John Paul II's "domestic" policy within the church is ambivalent. And out on the highways and byways, in villages and cities alike, the priesthood in local Catholic parishes is in crisis, as will be further examined in chapter 5.

The pontificate of John Paul II has been an enigma. The true meaning of it will be assessed only many years hence. In his message to the church on the occasion of the millennium, *Novo Millennio Ineunte*, (At the start of the new millennium), John Paul struck an optimistic note. He encouraged Catholics to "cast out into the deep" (recalling Christ's injunction to the apostles Peter and Andrew fishing on Lake

Galilee in Luke 5:4), to widen their nets, and to look forward to the future with confidence. He recalls the Jubilee of the year 2000, in the course of which he engaged in a "purification of memory" by requesting forgiveness of the church's past faults and welcomed thousands of pilgrims to Rome. He applauded the advances in ecumenism that have taken place and pledged the church to the pursuit of inter-religious dialogue in the new millennium. No other pope in history has expressed contrition for past failings in the church to the extent that he has, and few can have remained unmoved by his dramatic gesture of sorrow at the Wailing Wall of Jerusalem. It remains to be seen, however, if the church can now enter a period where concrete amends will be made to its own victims.

In his message for the World Youth Day, 2002, the pope invites youth to become "morning watchmen" and to "read the signs of the times" in the light of the gospel. But there are certain "signs" that youth are not allowed to read, for if they do read them, they point in a direction away from the Catholic Church. I have encountered several young Catholic women who are called to priesthood, but any "signs of the times" that direct young women to seek their vocation as a priest within the Catholic Church will not be included in the discussions for World Youth Day.

Despite the apparent expansiveness and openness to dialogue contained in his optimistic message for the new millennium and for World Youth Days, the pope still reasserts the unassailable rights of the Catholic Church to carry on as if the world in general, and plural-ist modern cities such as Toronto, the location for the 2002 World Youth Day, are still mission territories, ripe for conversion to the one, true Catholic Church. Other religions, he states in *Novo Millennio Ineunte,* are not bearers of God's revelation in and of themselves, but are imperfect and unreliable mirrors for a Christian image of God. Dialogue with other religions "cannot be understood as negotiation" and "the Church cannot forgo her missionary activity." The bark of Peter may be relaunching itself into this new millennium, but it's still in battleship mode.

John Paul II's vibrant personality and communication skills have called forth the world's admiration. So the media flock to the specta-cle of papal events, yet by and large, they disregard the substance of his message. This is not because of ill will, but because the truths that the Vatican speaks are still wrapped up in the garb of dishonored ide-ologies from the past. A reiteration of traditional Catholic positions on subjects such as religious pluralism, gender, sexuality, and the use of authority in the church that have gone unchallenged in past centuries is inadequate to meet the challenge of postmodern society.

The papal theology of the past thirty years has demonstrated many profound insights into the human condition. It has been packaged and delivered, though, in the form of an intellectual blueprint that retains unmistakable traces of discredited totalitarian papal ideology. The Catholic Church, which has been severely compromised by glaring errors of judgment in the past, can no longer escape from the contingency, uncertainty, and tragedy of the postmodern world into simplistic solutions offered by unquestioned authority. John Paul II may have asked forgiveness for the church's persecution of Galileo, but there is no indication that this has resulted in a more cautious approach within the church to the promulgation of so-called "universal" truths today. There often appears, as in the case of recent debates over stem cell research, to be a breathless rush into hasty answers to complex questions before the full dimensions of the questions have even become apparent. The mistakes of the past have not resulted in a chastened disposition toward a rigorous self-criticism, let alone humility, within the Vatican.

But the vigorous reassertion of papal authority has found favor in many quarters. John Paul II's vision of a reinvigorated, assertive Christendom has provided a rallying cry for many, both inside and outside the Catholic Church, who feel threatened by the world. A world in which the structures of privilege that have buttressed the power of white, Christian, male leadership are being dismantled is threatening to those who stood to gain the most from their privilege. Anglican clergy in England who opposed the decision of their church to ordain women have been welcomed with open arms into the Catholic fold. The Catholic Church in recent years has found enthusiastic allies among evangelical Protestant groups who would also prefer that Christianity stay anchored in the shelter of its patriarchal port rather than set out onto the open seas of the postmodern world. The Catholic hierarchy in the United States has recently been cajoled into an uneasy partnership with the fundamentalist Protestant revival that propelled George Bush into the presidency.

The postmodern transition from a universal system of ethics as defined by the narrow experience of a particular group of men in power toward more tentative positions that respect the particular experiences of all human individuals or groups is one that has been vigorously resisted by John Paul II. This is in spite of the fact that the Second Vatican Council began the deconstruction of the exercise of power in the church and the move toward a less belligerent and more consensus-seeking approach to the modern world. The documents of Vatican II did open up new perspectives for the renewal of the church but failed to supply new theological language and idioms to express this new vision. The result in the intervening years since the council has been that reactionaries within the church have tried to "take back" the council by interpreting its texts according to a preconciliar theological perspective. Those who have attempted to continue the work of the council by using its teaching as a springboard toward a new language and idiom for dialogue with the contemporary world have discovered themselves bogged down in an impasse. Liberation theology, feminist theology, Asian theology — all manifestations of this creative thrust of the Vatican II toward renewal through dialogue with the world rather than restoration — are threatened by the deadening impact of constant suspicion from Rome and misrepresentation by traditionalists.

Another problem which has hindered efforts to continue the renewal of the church begun at Vatican II is a procedural one. While the drafts of the council's documents were fresh working papers drawn up by mixed commissions of progressive theologians as well as bishops, the more conservative bishops then made so many amendments to the documents on the council floor that many documents became watered down by escape clauses inserted in the texts. These have since enabled Rome to present its restorationist agenda as consonant with the council's thinking. An example of this is the council's redefinition of the church as the People of God and its deliberate blurring of the distinction between priests and lay people. The conservatives managed to insert amendments to a later chapter in the same document that defined the church as a hierarchical structure. The result has been that the much-needed internal reform of the church has now come to a standstill.

HOW MUCH OF THE REVERSAL of Vatican II has resulted from deliberate papal intervention? Cardinal Karol Wojtyla, the future John Paul II, had been consecrated archbishop of Krakow, Poland, in 1958 and attended the council only sporadically. He participated little in the most controversial debates on the modernization of the liturgy, ecumenism, the partnerships of bishops and pope, and the new understanding of the church as primarily communitarian, as People of God rather than a hierarchically perfect society. Growing up in Poland in the early part of the twentieth century, the young Karol Wojtyla was raised in a culture that had experienced neither the reformation nor the democratic revolutions which had shaped the philosophy and politics of the rest of Europe and North America. Placed on the defensive by the impact of the atheistic communist revolution, Catholic philosophers and theologians in Poland remained largely untouched by the influence of the new streams of thought emerging in postmodern Europe.

John Paul II's early studies in philosophy had immersed him in the philosophical system known as phenomenology, the legacy of Max Scheler and Edmund Husserl. Phenomenologists approach the definition of truth through an analysis of lived experience. In this view, human experience of truth is not just a rational abstraction. It is also inseparable from emotion. It is thus never neutral, always contextual, and always influenced by attraction or repulsion of some kind. Although ethical values, for example, may be claimed to be objective, people form their values through experience as well as through intellect. From the earliest of his dissertations through the plethora of his later writings as pope, one can discern the influence of phenomenology in Wojtyla's effort to incorporate a respect for experience into dogmatic teachings. This had the potential to mark an improvement in the abstract, scholastic approach to ethics that has characterized so much of Catholic morality. But because John Paul's experience of democracy, a pluralistic society, and women, for example, has been extremely limited, his teaching has lacked a truly "catholic" approach to life.

His experience of family life was tragically marred by the death of his mother when he was nine years old. He was raised in an all-male household. During his four years of manual labor under the Nazis, while he also performed with an underground theater group in Krakow, prior to entering the seminary Karol Wojtyla never experienced an adult relationship with a woman. The wrenching give and take of deeply committed sexual relationships and the jagged edges of joy and sorrow which come with birthing and raising children have not formed part of his emotional development. It is for this reason that I believe his writings on sexuality and particularly on women, while they may be idealistic in their approach to feminine nature, lack concrete grounding in real life and an appreciation of the diversity

of women's personalities and experience. This may also account for
the fact that his prolific writings on sexuality and womanhood have
failed to convince all but a small minority of Catholics.

Second, he seems never to have been able to overcome a profound pessimism about the postmodern, secular world. After losing
his mother in 1929, ten years later he saw his motherland, Poland,
fall to Nazi occupation in 1939. One tyranny was followed immediately by another, when the communists took over the government
at the end of World War II in 1945. Religion, the Catholic Church,
Polish national resistance — all of these then became idealized and
fused into a deeply conservative outlook forged by years of brave
and tragic, but ultimately ineffectual, resistance to tyranny. Poland's
days of past glory were intimately bound up with the influence of
the Catholic Church. The Polish and Catholic nationalism in which
Wojtyla was raised owed much to a traditional and often romanticized interpretation of Catholic values. It became his bulwark of
resistance to the tyranny of both Nazism and communism. When adherence to a certain set of values has been forged in the school of great
suffering, as it was in his case, it becomes extremely hard ever to subject those values to internal critique. Changing those values threatens
the foundation of the moral order that has served to prevent an individual's descent into chaos. I believe that a deeply ingrained fear of
change as the harbinger of chaos or a descent into moral relativism
has colored John Paul's response to progressive movements in the
church and in society.

His formative early adulthood was marked by the idealism of Polish resistance, a mystical transcendence of the present into the eternal
world, a system of unchanging values, and a deep Marian piety. All
of these served as vehicles to transcend his concrete experience of
a world of tyranny and oppression and one that lacked feminine
influence. In his writings, Karol Wojtyla continued to interpret the
writings of the philosopher Husserl through a lens of transcendental
idealism. Unfortunately, Wojtyla removed Husserl's emphasis on experience from the concrete area of lived experience and emotion into
the realm of abstract spiritual ideals. The phenomenology of experience, in John Paul's writings, became subsumed into Aristotelian and
Thomist metaphysics of supernatural order and hierarchical control.
His writings are colored with a suspicion of the corporeal, the sexual,
and the irrational loss of control in orgasm. The body must always be
held in check. Sexual intercourse must be tempered by parenthood

and never used as a source of pleasure in its own right. This transcendental trajectory permeates John Paul II's writings and infects his teachings on sexuality with an air of unreality.

Karol Wojtyla's first doctoral dissertation, prepared at the Angelicum in Rome with the doctoral degree conferred by the Jagiellonian University in Krakow, concerned the phenomenology of mysticism viewed through the writings of John of the Cross. I find this of particular interest because in early adulthood I too was attracted by the mysticism of John of the Cross, and his writings have remained one of my favorite sources for prayer. But I find myself unable to relate to Wojtyla's analysis of the phenomenon of mysticism.[4] He argues that the mystical experience combines both the intellectual and emotional aspects of faith, but that the experience of mysticism is ultimately objective and devoid of emotional content. According to him, the mystic experience of God must be an utter abstraction beyond thought or emotion.

According to mystical theology, God is greater than all of reality combined and cannot be captured by either rational thought or emotion. God initiates the mystical experience by drawing the one who prays into an experience of the divine. This experience is one of being taken out of oneself by being part of a connectedness to all that is. But this is a profoundly emotional and profoundly moving experience. It is no accident that many of the classical mystical writers — John of the Cross himself, his friend and contemporary Teresa of Avila, as well as Catherine of Siena to name only a few — have described their experience of prayer in erotic terms. The total connectedness of prayer can be physically orgasmic. The spirit's total openness to God can resound in great spasms within the body, which are similar to multiple orgasms in sex.

Both mysticism and sex can lead to a connection with the orgasmic energy of love, which fuels the universe. For God is at once transcendent and beyond reality, but at the same time immanent and within reality. Not either-or but both-and. And the result, the orientation of both mysticism and of erotic love, is ultimately toward universal compassion. The connectedness of prayer and the ecstasy of sexual union both lead ultimately to a desire to foster the oneness of all creation. The experience of the transcendent, the being pulled out of oneself into something of ultimate otherness, leads the mystic and the lover back into a deep experience of connectedness with all of God's great world.

But in past centuries prayer, like every other aspect of Catholic life, became hierarchically ordered. Only celibates, monks, nuns, or priests were considered worthy of initiation into mysticism because the spiritual and the sexual were considered mutually exclusive. Lay people could say the rosary and attend Mass but were not considered capable of rising to the heights of contemplation. The eroticism of divine experience was interpreted by celibates within controlled, safe, and purely spiritual, idealistic terms. But now the linking of corporeal and spiritual eroticism is one of the great gifts that contemporary feminism has brought back into the Western church. The writings of Wojtyla, in many ways an admirable and accomplished philosopher, are flawed by his inability to critique and deconstruct the dualistic tension between matter and spirit that pervades scholastic philosophy. Even today, his moral exhortations see sexuality, unless tempered by procreation, as inimical to the life of the Spirit and the dedicated life of the celibate as superior to one lived through sexually expressed commitment.

JOHN PAUL II has an elevated sense of the burden of his office. His encyclical *Veritatis Splendor,* or *The Splendor of Truth,* published in 1993 represents his attempt to draw secure and impenetrable boundaries around the truth. Some commentators on the right wing of the church have hailed it as one of the greatest compendiums of thought to come out of the modern church. Others view this as a futile effort to close the stable door after the horse has bolted. When Galileo published his findings on cosmology, the church tried to squeeze the round universe back into a flat-earth theory. In *Veritatis Splendor* and in other writings, John Paul seems to be attempting to bottle the divergent streams of postmodern thought back into a narrow funnel of Roman revisionism. The foundational belief that animates *Veritatis Splendor* is that universal truths can be defined by virtue of unquestionable authority. This has become less and less credible, even to Catholics. Much as many respect the sincerity of the pope's motives, the Roman version of truth cannot be saved by ossifying it into unassailable concepts.

While an exalted view of the papal office as arbiter of global morality may appear pure, splendid, and rational to some restorationists, the articulation of truth inside and outside the church can no longer rest on a medieval construct of omnipotent papal jurisdiction. John Paul II and his supporters seem to have an absolute trust in his competence, which they believe is graced by the special endowment of the Holy Spirit that pertains to the papal office. The shadow side of this trust in absolute papal power is a distrust of the notion of collegiality (the sharing of Rome's authority with the world's bishops) and an apoplectic intolerance for theologians who are not in full agreement with him. *Veritatis Splendor* is an attempt to bring theologians into line with papal teaching on morality, particularly on contraception and abortion. For this reason it is worth detailed examination. It also provides an insight into the philosophical and theological foundations upon which the rest of John Paul's teaching is structured.

In the very first paragraph of the encyclical, a pessimistic notion of humankind as intrinsically oriented toward sin is introduced. The "original" sin of Adam and Eve, committed at the prompting of "Satan, the liar and the father of lies," has clouded humanity's capacity to know the truth and weakened its will to submit to God. "Thus," the pope continues, using masculine pronouns, "giving himself over to relativism and skepticism he goes off in search of an illusory freedom apart from truth itself" (par. 1).[5] This pessimistic outlook on modern civilization, in particular a mistrust of its progress in extending universal human rights, has become a hallmark of the conservative revival in the church fostered by this pope. No sooner is the concept of "freedom" mentioned than it is followed by a caution about sin. Freedom is always suspect because it can be an occasion of sin. So any movement toward the extension of political freedom or democracy, for example, is viewed as potentially tainted with license. Women's rights influence them to abandon motherhood; gay rights will promote hedonism and undermine the traditional family.

Humanity's propensity to sin through the exercise of an overweening freedom must be kept firmly in check by the guidance of the church's authority. Throughout the two-thousand-year history of the Catholic Church, its leaders have supported autocratic and dictatorial governments such as that of Augusto Pinochet in Chile and been suspicious of mass populist movements such as that led by Pinochet's predecessor, Salvador Allende. Monarchy, rather than democracy, has been the Catholic Church's preferred form of state organization until very recently. John Paul II's commitment to the democratic Solidarity movement in Poland has not carried over into support for workers' movements or the extension of freedom of speech and conscience beyond the boundaries of Poland.

The pope and other traditionalists advocate a return to the values

of Christian civilization as a solution to the apparent moral anar-
chy of the West. Society could then be restructured by a return to
patriarchal control over women and children. The nuclear Christian
family, for them, is a paradigm of the hierarchical control that should
exist in the rest of society. But belief in a God who functions through
hierarchically ordered domination is no longer viable. Since Christ
himself has destroyed the foundation of power based on domination,
to advocate a system of personal or religious values constructed on a
foundation of hierarchical power denies the profound meaning of the
Christian story. But the Vatican and its allies continue to use God as a
sanction for what they name as the only "natural" system of law and
order in society which functions according to a hierarchy of dominance and submission. This last gasp of the culture of patriarchal
dominance is deeply threatened by the newly emerging postmodern
consciousness of global solidarity and inclusiveness. The struggle between, on the one hand, the radical inclusiveness of a democratic
respect for pluralism and diversity and, on the other, the views of the
select few men who claim to speak for God and rule in God's name
is the crux of the challenge to all Western religions seeking to come
to terms with the contemporary world.

Honed by his many years spent in combating the absolutism of
communist ideology, the pope has emerged with a combative version
of morality which is based on an ideology of absolutism — that of
unquestioned papal authority. Since the fall of communism in Poland,
in which he played such a pivotal role, John Paul II has become increasingly suspicious of the influence of Western democratic values.
To his chagrin, postcommunist Poland has not grown into the shining example of Catholic values that he envisaged. It has instead been
corrupted with values he views as inimical to the Polish church: feminism, individualism, and moral relativism. In response, he has sought
to crack down on theological exploration within the church and to
restore strict boundaries between church and world, between clergy
and laity, and between male and female. This is in order to prevent
what he views as evil influences from Western society seeping into the
church, not just in Poland but throughout the world.

It is in the Ten Commandments, states *Veritatis Splendor,* that humanity must find the basis of universal morality. Before analyzing the
pope's appeal to the Ten Commandments as the universal basis for
morality, it must be noted that the commandments treat women as
part of the property of men. In the tenth commandment, women are

lumped in with cattle and donkeys: "Thou shalt not covet thy neighbor's wife, slaves, house, cattle, donkeys *or anything else he owns*" (italics mine; Exod. 20:17). This glaringly anachronistic statement on the role of women passes without comment in the pope's document. There is no attempt in *Veritatis Splendor*, even by way of a footnote, to modify it with any reference to the contemporary context. This is an example of John Paul's approach to truth which is based in a transcendent world, not the real world. It illustrates the absence of sensitivity in papal teaching as to the impact this kind of omission will have on women. It appears not to have occurred to him that women might take offense at being generically subsumed into "man's chattels."

John Paul II uses the Ten Commandments to construct an apparently unassailable argument for the authority of the Catholic magisterium. In fact it turns out to be a circular argument that goes like this. First, God set forth his laws in the Ten Commandments. Then Jesus came to expound these further. Jesus founded a church, the Catholic Church, which became the only conduit through which God is revealed to all people for all time. "Christ's relevance for all time is shown forth in his body, which is the Church" (par. 25). Christ gave the apostles power over the church. The Spirit of God released at Pentecost was given primarily to the twelve apostles. The direct successors of the twelve apostles are the bishops, headed by Peter, whose successor is the pope. Therefore the popes and bishops have a direct line to the Holy Spirit, to Jesus, and to God while that of the rest of the world is only indirect. Case closed. "The task of interpreting these prescriptions was entrusted by Jesus to the Apostles and their successors with the special assistance of the Spirit of Truth: 'He who hears you hears me' (Luke 10:16) so that they can know the answer to every question in every age." Their teaching consists of a take-it-or-leave-it attitude: "And ever since Apostolic times the Church's pastors have unambiguously condemned the behavior of those who fostered division by their teaching or by their actions" (par. 26).

This is a violent and blind attitude toward truth which betrays a woeful ignorance of the way traditional teachings have evolved within the church. It brooks no criticism or even nuances of interpretation by anyone outside the closed circle of authority. It also omits any inclusion of the heritage of Jewish teachings on the Ten Commandments as relevant to an appraisal of their value as universal norms of ethics.

Earlier in the document, the pope refers to his closed male circle of advisors in the Vatican as "experts in humanity" (par. 3). The universality of the moral truth proclaimed by the pope's circle of "experts in humanity" is to apply not just to Catholics, but to the whole of humanity for all time. "At all times but particularly in the last two centuries the popes and bishops have developed moral teaching . . . and contributed to a better understanding of moral demands in the areas of human sexuality, the family . . . and in the history of humanity their teaching represents a constant deepening of knowledge" (par. 4). The moral codes laid down in the Bible "must be faithfully kept and continually put into practice in the various different cultures throughout the course of history" and "the task of interpreting these prescriptions was entrusted by Jesus to the Apostles and their successors."

The source of its claim to hegemony over the moral life of all humanity is based on the Vatican's notion of natural law. The idea of natural law is derived from Aristotle and came into Catholic tradition through the writings of Thomas Aquinas. According to Aquinas's teaching on natural law, God has implanted a kind of built-in homing device within each person that directs his or her conscience toward the truth and the good, regardless of whether or not the person believes in God. God's universal precepts of truth and goodness can be arrived at through the use of human reason, without any help from religion.

But through a fallacious and closed circular argument, this universal prereligious and areligious bond between humanity and God becomes neatly packaged in *Veritatis Splendor* into another branch of the authority of Catholic popes and bishops. The line of reasoning is as follows (see par. 44). This universal natural law originates in God. God revealed the Ten Commandments to Moses. God then became human in the person of Jesus. Since God took so much trouble to explain the Law through Moses and Jesus, God must have meant this revelation to include and incorporate all that can ever be known before or since by human reason alone. "Man is able" states the pope, "to . . . discern good from evil by his reason, *in particular by his reason enlightened by Divine Revelation and by faith*, through the law which God gave . . . beginning with the commandments on Sinai" (par. 44). Natural law and divine law are effectively rendered indistinguishable. Ergo there is no other source of valid ethical reasoning outside the Catholic Church's interpretation of the commandments given to

Moses. So the Catholic Church emerges as the sole depository of the total sum of divine revelation and the interpreter of conscience and natural law for the whole world. This view is at the root of the Holy See's claim to advise the United Nations on all issues of morality.

This is not the only example in this encyclical where natural law is subsumed into divine law. Although the pope acknowledges the "imperative character" and supreme authority of conscience as a guide for individual judgment and action, the truth that conscience arrives at is always described as part of the divine law which the church already possesses. It is as though the Catholic Church is always waiting in the wings to pounce on an unwary seeker after truth. "Freedom of conscience is never freedom 'from' the truth but always and only freedom 'in' the truth . . . the Magisterium brings to light truths which [conscience] ought already to possess" (par. 45).

In the new Code of Canon Law, dissent from the church's teaching is criminalized and subject to automatic excommunication.[6] The traditional teaching on the duty of a Catholic to oppose and dissent in conscience from an erroneous teaching of the magisterium is suppressed. If this view had applied in former centuries, anyone who had spoken out against papal sanctioning of the Crusades, slavery, and the killing of heretics, or to the Catholic Church's vehement opposition to women's suffrage at the beginning of the twentieth century, would have been condemned and excommunicated, as indeed many lay Catholics were. The result of these exaggerated claims is a line of argument that rests ultimately only on authority. It infantilizes the adult conscience and ignores the experience of believers and nonbelievers alike. Its claim to universal moral objectivity is fatally marred not only on the surface by its use of exclusively male language, but at a deeper level by exclusively male experience and referencing. It is no longer possible for only one-half of humanity to speak with authority on the totality of human thought and experience.[7]

The pope has often stated that the winds of change do not pertain to the doctrinal realm. Papal teaching floats somehow in a sublime abstract realm, untarnished by history and the evolution of human understanding of the truth. But if there had never been any development of doctrine Catholics would still be allowed to own slaves and forbidden to use a bank.[8]

Any enlightenment by "natural reason" of non-Catholics outside the church is also now regarded as flawed, even though Vatican II acknowledged that the Spirit of God often works to transform the world ahead of the church, the idea of religious liberty and freedom of conscience being a case in point. The Thomist idea that the person (and Thomas understood only men to be fully human persons) exists in a state of static and unchanging moral awareness can no longer be sustained in the face of developments in medicine, psychology, and other social sciences. The notion that a person is always in evolution, on a lifetime pilgrimage toward the destination of loving union with God and with neighbor is not only more consonant with contemporary thought, but also resonates with the gospel values lived and taught by Jesus. Few people have been as careless of static, orthodox formulas as Jesus was, writes Bailie. "Jesus was crucified by people who were afraid that doctrinal mistakes were being made and that some false religion was going to lay waste the world," and "in both life and death, Jesus was opposed by the most respected institutions of this world."[9]

It is clear from this encyclical that papal teaching is still beholden to a greater extent to the secular concept of natural law, derived from Aristotle by Thomas Aquinas, than to the gospel message of Christ in all its richness and ambiguity. But the natural law that is envisaged in *Veritatis Splendor* is not even understood, as it was by Aquinas, as the inner enlightening of our hearts and minds by God so that we have a propensity toward good rather than evil. The pope's notion of natural law is a code of behavior, especially when it comes to sexual ethics, that lays down detailed norms of particular actions, such as contraception.

The reality is that even though freedom of conscience is understood to be guaranteed under natural law, in the Vatican's eyes individual conscience lacks moral autonomy: "an autonomy conceived in this way also involves the denial of a specific doctrinal competence on the part of the Church and her magisterium with regard to particular moral norms" (par. 37). The encyclical also condemns the position adopted by some Catholic theologians that there is a distinction between a "fundamental option" toward good and the individual actions of a person in a particular and limited context. The idea of the "fundamental option" is derived from the teaching of the Jesuit theologian Karl Rahner, adapted from the philosophy of Jacques Maritain. According to Rahner, the morality of an individual act should be assessed with reference to the theological and psychological depths within the person rather than simply fitting into an external list of mortal sins (fatally serious and deserving of hell) and venial sins (not so serious) with automatic penalties attached.[10] In this view, persons who think deeply about the direction of their lives and have oriented themselves toward consistently ethical behavior have made a fundamental option for the "good." This ethical disposition toward goodness can grow and mature with experience or it can decline with neglect of regular self-appraisal. But to be truly ethical, it must be arrived at in freedom.

Every moral choice, then, that confronts a person in the course of daily life is a reflection of this fundamental option, but each individual choice does not necessarily amount to an abrogation of the fundamental option. A decision not to give a donation to a person begging on the street on a particular day, for example, even though this is in direct contravention of the words of Jesus, who tells us that it is he himself who comes to us in the poor and needy (Matt. 25), does not necessarily represent a fundamental option for selfishness. But if the person who refused the donation is then influenced by friends or by the media to accept uncritically that the poor are always lazy and prone to crime and then decides she will never again help a street person, this would eventually result in a hardening of her heart and a change in her fundamental option from good to evil.

So the fundamental option or orientation of a person's life is not changed in and of itself by one individual action, though it can be changed for good or evil by a series of actions. Those who believe in the idea of a fundamental option therefore hold that a person cannot be eternally damned on the basis of one individual action unless such an action is the result of a serious, deliberate pattern signifying the rejection of God and neighbor. The principle put forward in this encyclical, which would condemn someone to automatic, eternal damnation on the basis of a purely external judgment of the objective guilt of one individual action, represents an approach to ethics that is devoid of compassion for the complex circumstances in which people actually live.

Certain actions, according to *Veritatis Splendor,* are always wrong regardless of the particular circumstances in which they were committed or the general circumstances and experiences of the person who acts. Contraception and abortion are ipso facto considered mortally sinful. There are no mitigating circumstances, such as rape in war or the likelihood of a fatal exposure to AIDS that could serve as an exception to mitigate the sin of these actions.

In the seventeenth century, several popes declared that to believe in the theory of a sun-centered universe was a mortal sin. In the eighteenth century, according to the papacy, it was reading the Bible that would send Catholics to hell. In the nineteenth century, freedom of conscience, freedom of the press, and freedom of religion were all declared by various popes to be mortal sins.[11] In the light of these historical blunders, it might be assumed that the Vatican would adopt a more cautious and prudent approach to itemizing today's mortal sins in detail. The proclamation of universal teachings on ethics in *Veritatis Splendor* lacks any historical perspective on the evolution of Vatican teachings. This pope's lack of historical perspective in his teaching on sin betrays a blindness to its own very particular cultural context. John Paul II presents his teaching as an objective, rational, and transhistorical analysis of human sexuality. But what he presents as universal is in reality a series of propositions on sexual norms as these appear compelling to members of the celibate Catholic clergy.[12] Masturbation, contraception, and abortion are stated to be always and in every circumstance intrinsically evil in and of themselves. No context, not even the avoidance of death, can ever change the most severe application of the law in these cases.

The pope equates a more compassionate reasoning on contraception, for example, with a simple idea that it teaches that "the end justifies the means." He rejects a priori any arguments that do not support the intrinsic evil of every contraceptive act. In practice, though, the church permits contraception. Nuns in danger of rape have been issued the contraceptive pill. Many nuns and other women who have been made pregnant by priests have also been forced to undergo abortions: the priests have not been held responsible.

The spread of AIDS provides another more concrete case in point. A compassionate solution to this problem would be to see that in this context, the use of contraceptives in sexual intercourse is motivated by the avoidance of death rather than the prevention of birth. The contraceptive nature of the sexual act is a secondary effect of the morally correct intention to prevent death.

But the Catholic Church has stood firmly against this line of reasoning, insisting that the only way to prevent death from AIDS is for a couple, even in marriage, to practice total and permanent abstinence from sex. This kind of cold legalism in the face of human suffering is an indication of the lengths to which John Paul II has been willing to go to subject truth to the exigencies of preserving papal power in

the church. A central platform of the restorationist papacy of John
Paul II has been an attempt to revive that discredited 1968 encyclical *Humanae Vitae* of Paul VI, in which all forms of contraception
are condemned. Many Catholic bishops at the time *Humanae Vitae*
was issued tried to soften its impact by calling for the flexibility of a
"pastoral solution" and appealing to the primacy of conscience. But
in *Veritatis Splendor*, the pope condemns any pastoral solution in any
field of sexual ethics as "a challenge to the very identity of the moral
conscience in relation to human freedom and God's law" (par. 57).
As Gil Bailie has pointed out in his expansion on the ideas of René
Girard examined in earlier chapters, the more widespread the questioning of the old mythology becomes, the more intensive the efforts
become of its proponents to defend it by shoring up their authority.
The cumulative effect of this overwhelming demand renders the cultural leaders of the tradition insensitive to the dangerous fragility of
the credibility on which their authority now rests.[13] *Veritatis Splendor*
is a case in point.

The encyclical ends with a eulogy of Mary as "Mother of Mercy"
(par. 118). The pope's intention here may have been to end on a more
pastoral note. But the stereotype of Mary as the nurturing, loving, and
compassionate mother of Jesus undermines this intent. Mary is held
up as a model of self-giving and acceptance, a passive and obedient
stereotype of femininity who exemplifies the pope's idealization of
woman's nature. Woman is the one who is the softening influence in
the hard lives of men and the one who is supposed to teach men how
to be good by their own example of self-abnegation. Moral freedom,
for Mary, meant "giving herself to God" and "accepting God's will."

This is dangerous ground. How far is the self-abnegation of
women's interests and the submerging of their personalities into this
project of redeeming men to extend? And is not the compassion of
Jesus and his forgiving and loving nature the model for all Christian
discipleship, male and female, rather than the motherhood of Mary,
which is gender-specific to women? It is hard not to exercise what
feminist theologians call the "hermeneutic of suspicion" here and to
see reference to motherhood as an extension of the pope's anthropol-
ogy of different human natures of men and women. Jesus is never
proclaimed in papal documents as a male example of meekness.

Women have not hitherto possessed the social and religious power
to shape the church's tradition: their input is absent from the church's
memory and experience. The church even today does not acknowledge

the moral agency of women as subjects of their own moral lives. Instead of attempting to remedy this by incorporating women into
decision-making positions in the church, the Vatican has insisted with
the full weight of infallibility that they be barred from ordination. The
pope's description of the "motherhood" of the church as integrally
linked with Mary's feminine obedience and docility means that this
encyclical ends, as it began, on a jarringly sexist note.[14]

Papal views on sexual morality, which have been so strongly emphasized in papal teachings such as *Veritatis Splendor* over the past
twenty years, are not merely matters for abstract debate among bishops and theologians. They affect millions of Catholics throughout the
world, and they reach deeply into the personal lives of believers.

As a teacher in a Catholic school, I have encountered the rami-
fications of these teachings on an almost daily basis. The absolute
ban on contraception and abortion has resulted in a prohibition of
the provision of any information on these topics to adolescents in
Catholic schools.

In my first year of teaching in a Catholic school, Tracy, one of the
girls in my Grade 11 Religion class, became pregnant. She was fifteen
years old. Tracy was adamantly opposed to having an abortion but
knew that her parents would not let her keep the baby. She confided
to me that she had decided to leave home for the duration of the
pregnancy and seek shelter in one of the Catholic group homes that
supported teenagers in this predicament. I promised her my support in
this decision. Unfortunately, Tracy also confided in one of her friends.
This friend told her own mother, who was a friend of Tracy's mother.
She talked to Tracy's mother and so the secret was out. The upshot
was that Tracy's parents made an appointment for her at an abortion
clinic and escorted her there themselves on the day of the abortion.
Would Tracy be subject to excommunication and eternal damnation
for this act? How responsible was she for having the abortion? Should
she have run away anyway and take the risk of herself and her baby
ending up on the street, as happens to many young single mothers?

At another Catholic school I was placed in charge of the dropout
prevention alternative program. The girls in the program were at risk
of dropping out of school, usually because of behavioral or family
problems. They were placed in a small class in an intensely supportive atmosphere. As their teacher for the better part of the day, I
also became their confidante and often provided a shoulder to cry on

and liberal doses of hugs. Several of the girls in the program became pregnant over the course of the year. One of them, Carmela, had a particularly difficult set of experiences.

Carmela was born in Brazil. She was seven years old when her parents separated and she and her sister were abandoned. The two ended up on the street in Rio de Janeiro but were rescued and taken to an orphanage. Carmela's mother eventually traced them, and a few years later the three of them emigrated to Canada. Carmela's mother became involved in an abusive relationship, and the girls were then placed in foster care. Carmela moved in with a couple, Diane and Joseph. It was at this stage, at age fifteen, that she came into my class. A year earlier Carmela had begun a sexual relationship with Rui, a twenty-eight-year-old married man. She did not tell me how they originally became involved, but it was a consensual relationship. Rui was in the habit of using a condom but forgot it on a number of occasions. Hence her pregnancy.

When she told Rui that she was pregnant, he reacted by telling her that if she had the baby and it became known that he was the father, he would be charged with having sex with a minor. He would then be imprisoned and then deported back to Portugal because he did not hold Canadian citizenship. (Whether or not this would actually have happened is a moot point, but he convinced Carmela that it was a possibility.) Carmela was under enormous pressure from him to have an abortion. Although she had kept her foster mother, Diane, in ignorance of the relationship with Rui, I persuaded Carmela to tell her about it to see if Diane would support her for the duration of the pregnancy and then through the birth. Then the baby could be given up for adoption.

But Diane was adamant that Carmela did not have the emotional stability or psychological maturity to carry this pregnancy to term. She argued in favor of abortion. Carmela had the abortion seven weeks into the pregnancy. Was this, in terms of Vatican thinking, an intrinsically evil action on her part, one so heinous as to warrant automatic excommunication from the church and, consequently, eternal damnation if she does not repent before her death?

There are a number of ethical issues involved in Carmela's situation. There is the status of the personhood of the fetus as compared with that of the mother. There is the freedom of conscience of Carmela and the effect of the pressure placed on her from other sources. Whether the pope wants to face it or not, abortion is part of the context of the lives of women all over the world. The church's teaching as it presently stands is far too simplistic a framework for the plurality of the contexts of women's lives and the complicated social and emotional issues bound up with sexuality and pregnancy. Late-term abortions frequently involve Catholic women who have avoided making a decision to terminate the pregnancy any earlier because of fear of the consequences of disobeying the church and of causing scandal in often conservative Catholic families. "There are no short cuts to a Catholic abortion-free Promised Land," says Catholic commentator Clifford Longley.[15] The trial and imprisonment or fining of doctors, nurses, and social workers who assist women in obtaining abortions is still a fact in conservative Catholic countries such as Portugal. Forty-two women were recently condemned under that country's rigid abortion laws.[16]

It is only in the past 150 years that Catholic teaching on the morality of abortion has accorded the fetus the same rights as the adult human being. Until very recently, abortion was classified in the church as a sin of sex rather than a sin of homicide.[17] A decisive change in this view occurred with the Declaration of the Immaculate Conception of Mary in 1854. The doctrine of the Immaculate Conception of Mary (not to be confused with Mary's virginal conception of Jesus) teaches that Mary was "conceived without original sin" by her parents, Joachim and Anne. In other words, even though Mary was conceived in the normal way through sexual intercourse between her parents, she was not born under the curse of Adam and Eve, which, as St. Augustine taught, is transmitted through sex. In traditional Catholic teaching, the curse of Adam and Eve has resulted in all their descendants being born with a tendency toward sin, which can be erased only through the sacrament of baptism. In other words, Mary was sinless from the moment of her conception. This implies, then, that she must have had a soul since the moment of her conception.

Until Pius IX made a dogmatic statement about abortion in 1869, the majority of Catholic theologians and the Council of Trent itself (1545–63) had accepted some form of delayed hominization, or human personhood, for the fetus. A distinction was made between the unformed and the fully formed fetus. Hominization, in this view, did not occur until the fetus was fully formed. And so Gratian, the church's first canon lawyer, could write, "The one who brings about an abortion before the soul is infused into the body is not a murderer."[18] But in 1869, Pope Pius IX, the pope of the Immaculate Conception, issued a declaration that ensoulment occurs at conception. He made abortion grounds for automatic excommunication — even the abortion of an ectopic pregnancy.[19]

Some conservative Catholics now hold that a newly fertilized egg should have the same rights from the moment of conception as a full human being, child or adult, so that the law should give even the non-implanted embryo the same status in law and morality as its mother. They condemn even the "morning-after pill" as equivalent to murder, a position rejected by the American Medical Association as lacking scientific foundation because pregnancy is defined from the moment of implantation. But if "pregnancy" actually begins with conception, then what of the millions of fertilized eggs that are spontaneously ejected by nature before implantation? If these too are fully human and the loss of each one is as tragic as, say, the crib death of a baby, why is there no church ritual for conditional baptism of a blastocyst or some kind of ceremony for the disposition of its remains? The fact is that the beginning of truly human life cannot be discerned at the moment of its conception. Nor has the "moment of conception" view of the initial bestowal of human personhood always been taught in Catholic tradition.

Augustine of Hippo, a theologian who wrote prolifically and in much detail about sexual matters, condemns abortion. But he condemns it not because he considers it equivalent to murder, but because it is an example of the perverse use of human sexuality. In Augustine's view sex, even between married couples, is justifiable only if it is directed toward procreation. Sexual pleasure, even in marriage, is always tainted with sin. So all contraception, even what is known as the rhythm method, the one approved by the Catholic Church, is tantamount to a perversely lustful use of sexuality because it is not directed toward the primary purpose of marriage, i.e., conception. Augustine stated that a pregnant woman who has an abortion could not be accused of murder because the unformed fetus is not a full human being. But to procure an abortion is wrong nevertheless because it is an example of the fruit of a sinfully lustful use of sexuality.[20] Augustine describes abortion as the cutting of the fruit from the body — *ab orto* is the Latin root of the word — a position that relates to Aquinas's view of the vegetative state of the early fetus.

Thomas Aquinas taught that the fetus passes through three stages toward human personhood. He defined human personhood as ensoulment with a rational soul. This idea, known as the succession of souls, which was originally taught by the Stoics, passed via Aristotelian philosophy into the tradition of the church and remained the foundation of the church's teaching on abortion up to the mid-nineteenth century. According to Aquinas, the fetus passes through a vegetative state, followed by a sentient or animal state, and finally reaches its rational or human state. For Aquinas, this human personhood is based on the acquisition of human sentiency.

So a detailed examination of the teachings of Augustine and Aquinas demonstrates that Catholic teaching on abortion, like most other issues of morality, has undergone significant change and evolution. The fundamentalists in the pro-life movement argue that the teaching on the immediate hominization and ensoulment of the fertilized egg has been a traditional Catholic teaching since the beginning. But this is not historically correct. Aquinas insisted on the union of the rational soul and the body as a prerequisite for human personhood. The Council of Vienne confirmed this position, which is known as hylomorphism, in 1311 when it stated, "The rational soul is the essential form of the human body."[21]

More modern Thomists such as Joseph Donceel, S.J., support the idea of delayed hominization implicit in this hylomorphic conception of human personhood. Before the development of the central nervous system, the fetus does not bear the characteristics of rationality and sentiency, which occur with the joining of the cerebral cortex and the central nervous system around the middle of the second trimester. "Despite the body's potential as primary matter, there is no human person without the actualizing principle of the substantial form, the soul. The substantial form, or soul, can be present only in a body capable of receiving it, one which has developed beyond the earliest stages of pregnancy."[22]

In the late sixteenth century, the morality of abortion was still defined by virtue of the stage of formation of the fetus. Abortion of an "unformed" fetus was not considered murder, whereas that of a "formed" fetus was. In 1588, Pope Sixtus V attempted to resolve this by issuing a bull, *Effraenetum,* which stated that contraception and abortion were both homicides, a penalty for which was automatic excommunication, which could be lifted only by the pope himself. But three years later, Pope Gregory XVI reversed this, stating that "where no homicide or no animated fetus is involved, then the church should not punish more strictly than civil legislation does."[23] The church also taught that fetuses in danger of death should be baptized conditionally only if "there was reasonable foundation for admitting that they were animated by a rational soul."[24] Even today, the church does not insist on baptism in the case of the miscarriage of the fetus.

In the seventeenth century, with the dawn of scientific study of conception with the aid of a microscope, scientists such as Niklaas Hartsoeker (1656–1725) began to study the human sperm in detail. They initially thought they could detect the shape of a perfectly formed human being in miniature in each sperm.[25] Thus was born the idea of preformationism — that each sperm contained a tiny perfect human being, or "homunculus," just waiting to be deposited in the mother's womb and grow to full development as a person. Traces of the notion of preformationism are still apparent in the church's teaching on the sinfulness of masturbation. The spilling of the male seed is viewed as the wasting of thousands of potential human beings.

IN 1930, Pope Pius XI issued the encyclical *Casti Connubii* (Chaste spouses). It condemned abortion without exception. This teaching forms the basis of the present position on the absolute and unconditional "right to life" of the fetus. Based on the idea of immediate hominization, it holds that abortion is the equivalent of murder. But those who support this right to life of the conceptus no longer use arguments from a preformationist position. Today, the argument in favor of immediate human personhood is based on the presence of human genetic material in the conceptus. According to this view, the presence of human DNA in the fertilized egg indicates that a full human being is present from the moment of conception and therefore abortion at any stage of pregnancy is murder. But the pre-embryonic zygote does not possess the sufficient actualization of genetic information within its chromosomes to necessarily develop into a full embryo. And when the embryo does form at about three weeks, there is added information accrued from its maternal RNA. If identical twins have been conceived, the initially implanted embryo does not immediately subdivide into two potential human individuals.

While the fact of the presence of human DNA in the conceptus is not in dispute, there are other considerations to take into account in assessing its human personhood. The presence of human DNA indicates that it is human, as opposed to any other species of life. But is the form of that human life tantamount to real human personhood, which gives the conceptus as full a right to life as its mother? The church's current position on abortion calls for respect for human personhood "from the moment of conception." But what exactly is the "moment of conception" and when does it occur? Science has revealed that conception is a process, not a single moment. Fewer than one-third of all conceptions, i.e., fertilizations of human eggs, lead to the formation of a fetus. Nature aborts these early blastocysts at a high rate.

The argument against abortion from the point of view of the potentiality of the fetus smacks of determinism. It is based on the notion that a person is himself or herself from the moment of conception and set on an inevitable path of no return. But the fetus does not turn itself into a human being: it is dependent on the mother for its potentiality to become actual. The probability of personhood present in the fetus cannot be realized without considerable effort on the part of others. Modern scientific study of the physical development of the fetus does come close to full circle on Aquinas's idea of the evolution of human personhood, though for different reasons. The nerve cells which start to appear in the embryo after four weeks do not constitute a functional central nervous system. The brain, which starts forming at around fourteen weeks, is not operational until synapses start to appear at around twenty-four weeks.[26] Only toward the end of the second trimester can sentiency be said to occur. In countries where abortion is legal, 99 percent of all abortions take place before this stage.

The argument about the morality of abortion centers on differences of opinion about the essence of what constitutes human personhood. Traditional Catholic theology has taught that a human person is made up of a unity of rational and immortal soul with physical body. The nature and timing of this union of soul and body is at the heart of the debate about abortion. So is the argument about the right of the mother to choose whether or not to bear a child. Catholic theology to date has neglected to take into account the separate needs and interests of the mother. The freedom of choice of the woman to conceive and bear a child, so often negated in coercive sexual situations, is never alluded to in the church's teaching. In Catholic theology, the life of the conceptus or fetus always trumps or supersedes the right to life of the mother. The absolutism of the church's prohibition of abortion under any circumstances, its harsh treatment of women who have abortions, and its obdurate opposition even to the use of the "morning-after pill," fallaciously classified by the church as an abortifacient, is now being questioned.

The anti-abortion position is often framed in the context of the fifth commandment, "Thou Shalt Not Kill." Abortion, in this view, involves the deliberate murder of an innocent human being. So does war, especially in the nuclear age. And yet church teaching permits the killing of innocent human beings as "collateral damage" if the war in question is considered just. The U.S. Catholic bishops have publicly supported President George W. Bush's invasion of Afghanistan because, in their view, it falls under the traditional Catholic definition of a just war. It is interesting to note that at the same time that the U.S. bishops have adopted a more tolerant position on war, they have become more intolerant on abortion. The move toward support for the war in Afghanistan marks a shift away from the position adopted in their 1983 Pastoral Letter *On War and Peace*.[27] In this letter, the bishops state that "the possibility of taking even one human life is a prospect we should consider in fear and trembling."[28] They describe war, as St. Augustine did, as both the result of sin and the remedy for sin "which arises from disordered ambitions, but which could also be used, in some cases, to restrain evil and protect the innocent."

The traditional doctrine of the "just war" enunciated in Catholic teaching is based on two principles: a *jus ad bellum* (a just cause for war) and a *jus in bello* (just actions in war). According to this teaching, states can resort to war only if there is a real need to preserve the conditions necessary for human life; if it is declared by the competent authority; if it is waged for a just cause; and then only as a last resort after all other means of settling the dispute have been exhausted. The damage to be inflicted must also be proportionate to the good result intended. As for the *jus in bello*, this demands that the slaughter inflicted in war be limited and that the lives of innocent civilians should not be sacrificed. In a nuclear, technological age, the bishops stated in 1983, it is impossible to envisage a war that could fulfill these two last criteria, given the possibility of escalation of the conflict and the difficulty of confining the attack to military targets which do not involve civilian casualties. Twenty years later, the U.S. bishops have evidently had second thoughts on that position.

If the church still accepts the possibility of a "just war" where innocent civilians, including children, are to be regarded as "collateral damage," then it seems feasible that the church should consider the adoption of a "just abortion" theory. A pregnancy that results from rape or nonconsensual sex should be considered an act of aggression inflicted on an innocent person, and aborting the fetus as an act of self-defense on the part of the woman. If children and adults, whose full humanity is not in doubt, can be justifiably sacrificed in the course of war, then sacrificing the life of the fetus, whose full human status is less well established, could well be justified under certain circumstances. Abortion, furthermore, is often the last and only resort for women who lack access to contraception, sometimes as a direct result of opposition by the Catholic Church to the distribution of information and access to birth control.

I have to confess to profound ambivalence on the issue of abortion. In my twenties, I was theoretically convinced of the rightness of the Catholic Church's position and enrolled as a speaker for the Right to Life movement. But a combination of life experience and my encounters with women in a wide variety of situations, especially in parts of the world where poverty and discrimination prevail, has caused me to revise the rigidity of my former views. Further study of the scientific development of the fetus has also led me to adopt a more nuanced position on its full human personhood. I no longer accept the position that abortion in the early stages of pregnancy is the equivalent of murder. After years of thought, enlightened by this combination of new experience and knowledge, I have now achieved a position on the abortion issue that I can support with head and heart. The diversity and complexity of women's lives, their lack of freedom of choice in conception, and the horrendous conditions under which they may have to carry a pregnancy to term, as well as the lack of access to reliable family planning, are all part of the context in which women come to a decision on whether or not to carry a pregnancy to term. The Catholic Church's prohibition of contraception, even within marriage, is itself a direct cause of innumerable abortions. Catholic hospitals are forbidden to perform vasectomies, tubal ligations, or abortions, even in the case of rape or a threat to the life of the woman. In these days of government cutbacks and the downsizing of public health in the U.S. and Canada, the mergers of secular hospitals with Catholic hospitals has resulted in a decline in reproductive services to all women, whether Catholic or not.

Having conceived and nurtured two wonderful and wanted children in my own womb, I could never achieve a casual attitude toward abortion or one that presents it as just another means of contraception. I do not support access to abortion in the third trimester of pregnancy, except in the rare situation where the life of the mother is placed at risk by the continuation of the pregnancy. Up to about twenty-four weeks, hominization cannot be said to have taken place, and abortion should be legal and available without restriction up to this point. My experience of the harsh conditions of so many women's lives and my access to a more scientific knowledge about the development of the fetus has convinced me that safe, timely, and secure access to abortion is an essential right for women everywhere. To have an abortion can be a morally correct decision. Carmela, my student, made an ethically good decision. The teaching put forward in *Veritatis Splendor* and other papal writings to the effect that young women such as Tracy and Carmela face the possibility of eternal damnation as a result of their one act of procuring an abortion is incompatible with belief in a compassionate and loving God. It also betrays a total ignorance of the difficulties of their context and the pressures placed on them at the time when they arrived at their decisions.

In an ideal world, abortion would not be necessary. In that ideal world, all relationships would be loving. All relationships would be freely chosen and all children wanted. God, after all, gave Mary the mother of Jesus the choice on whether or not to become pregnant. God's pattern of dealing with human beings has always been pro-choice. In God's ideal world, all relationships would be based on equality between the genders as described in the story of creation in the first chapter of the Book of Genesis. In an ideal world, all women would be safe from rape and all forms of sexual assault, in times of war as well as in peace. All men would take an equal share in the responsibility for financing, nurturing, and raising their children. The means of regulating births by contraception as well as by Natural Family Planning would be free, accessible, and available without stigma or shame. Sex education for young men as well as women would cover the full range of options, including abstinence. And if poverty and disease for all children had been eliminated, *then* abortion would be extremely rare, and perhaps not even necessary.

Such an ideal world though is far from realization, but I believe that it is possible. That is why I continue to struggle for its achievement. And I continue to take issue with the Catholic Church because it has become an impediment to the achievement of such a world.

The tragedy of the present obsession in the Catholic Church with abortion as the only criterion of morality is that the influence of the pro-life movement within the church has paralyzed the wider discussion of public morality in society at large and fenced it in within the private, sexual realm. It has caused a shift within Catholicism worldwide into single-issue politics, where the proof of being a "true" Catholic is opposition to abortion. The teaching is always stated in the most extreme and absolutist terms, with no opportunity for discussion. Catholic politicians who favor the pro-choice position are increasingly under fire from reactionary Catholic groups. Even bishops can fall into the trap of the one-issue obsession with abortion. Bishop Fred Henry of Calgary told reporters in 2000 that he would deny a Catholic burial to Joe Clark, former prime minister of Canada and now leader of one of the opposition parties, if he did not abandon his pro-choice views.[29]

One of the main challenges facing John Paul II's successor will be to restore a sense of balance to the Catholic Church's pursuit of justice in the public, corporate realm as well as in the private and individual realm. This will mean a renewed emphasis on the common good as a goal of the state. At a time when the poor are being ravaged by rampant capitalism, and the environment is being degraded almost beyond repair, the prophetic voice of the Catholic Church has dwindled into querulous nagging about the rights of the fetus. Strategically this plays right into the hands of those forces on the right wing of both religion and politics that are placing the survival of all life on the planet at risk in their unfettered pursuit of profit and consumerism in the public arena. These same conservative groups who want the state to back out of regulating the economy also call for significant state intervention to enforce their view of private sexual morality and to outlaw abortion altogether. They have increasingly found common ground with the traditionalist lay Catholic groups, which have been founded and flourished during the papacy of John Paul II. The overweening emphasis on sexuality as the prime context for morality has also drawn the Catholic Church into close partnership with other reactionary groups in the Protestant churches and with theocratic Islamic nations.

All three of these former adversaries, Catholic, Protestant, and Muslim, are discovering common ground in their resistance to the advancement of women and the twisting of truth to serve the perpetuation of patriarchal power. This resurgence of fundamentalism, and the threat this poses to the equal rights of women as well as to the continuation of peaceful and pluralist co-existence will be one of the major challenges for the Catholic Church during the next papacy and beyond.

FOUR

The New Catholic and Protestant Religious Right

Dear Joanna, the letter began. *Thank you so much for your brave and truthful book.*[1] *I devoured it in one day and lay in bed late at night, thinking and reading. Memories and emotions washed over me. In my shift from conservative Catholicism, based on a yearning for obedience to 'orthodoxy' and also on self-doubt, to a liberal faith rooted in love and liberation, I have been searching for voices like yours.*

It was July 1999 when this letter arrived, from a Canadian woman in her early twenties who I will call Sara. After receiving the letter, I contacted Sara, and we arranged to meet. This young woman's keen intellect and remarkably accurate analysis of the church impressed me. Her letter continues:

...I believed that only in adherence to strict sexual morality, of the kind espoused by John Paul II and Catholic conservatives, lay the path of freedom and respect for women. As a child I wondered why girls couldn't become priests and why [one church] had altar girls when [another] didn't.... The privileges meted out to my brothers took a back seat in my consciousness, however, when I discovered that girls were not only not privileged; they were under sexual threat. I tried to suppress disloyal thoughts of my church and sexual morality. In my last year of high school I became involved in the Pro-Life-Pro-Chastity movement.

That way madness lay. While sexuality was no longer something hatefully sniggered at, it was something evil that could only be turned into good at the marriage altar by a priest. I suffered terribly in my attempts to be a "good girl." St. Maria Goretti, who chose death by stabbing over rape at knifepoint, was held out as an example of sexual goodness. The celibate Holy Family was, bizarrely, our model of family life. "Sanctity for Life," compassion for "babies and moms"

81

was never separated from a right-wing agenda: anti-condom, anti-Pill, anti-gay rights, and anti-feminist.

My friends joined Opus Dei while I stayed on the fringes, torn between the desire to be a feminist and a good daughter of the church. The young men in the movement divided women into groups of virgins, whores (feminists, "pro-aborts"), and mothers. We virgins were not proof against scorn, however. In my diaries of that era I have recorded a comment made by the son of a prominent pro-life activist to my friend: "Girls wear jewelry just to give themselves value."

... Sickened by the intolerance of pro-life adults and the sheer insanity of trying to convert my university to conservatism, I quit the pro-life movement. My respect for conservative morality remained, however. I married at twenty-five a man who prized my virginity more than he did me. After a year of escalating emotional and even sexual abuse, I did the unthinkable: I left and filed for divorce. The monsignor who had married us counseled that I had to stay to suffer the pain, the agony, and the humiliation because then at least I would know that I had tried. My parish priest, a liberal guy beaming with love, said, "Honey, get out while you're young." I heard the voice of Christ in his words and knew that God loved me and wanted me to be happy, not humiliated.

In the past two years, I have received comfort and help from my zany, liberal parish priest and my feminist Catholic therapist. I have begun to recognize that God loves sexuality, and that Christ's message of liberation from sin includes liberation from sexism. I think it was Mary Daly who said patriarchy is the world's religion. If this is true, it must be replaced by the love of God.

So thank you again, Joanna, for sharing your story and reading mine. Your book fills me with hope for the church we love so much. I dream of a day when all rank-and-file Catholics will stand up at Mass and say what we truly believe: that the majority of us in the West use birth control, that John Paul II's writing is incomprehensible to the laity, that God is not a man, and that the Catechism, translated to deliberately exclude the feminine, grievously insults and hurts at least half of God's people.

Sara's struggle, her inability to reconcile the orthodoxy of power with the truth that was coming to birth within her, is a poignant example of the dilemma faced by many young Catholics today. Intelligent, sensitive, spiritual, and trusting, they are trying to discover and to remain faithful to a truth that is life-giving but find themselves stifled in a church that will not allow them to spread their wings, explore their creativity, and grow up.

The movements Sara mentions, Opus Dei and Pro-Life, are just two of the many reactionary groups that have proliferated in the Catholic Church during the papacy of John Paul II. She encountered first hand the misogyny, the rigidly hierarchical obedience to authority, and the dysfunctional attitude to sexuality and relationships that characterize the Catholic and Protestant right. This is not how Jesus defined fidelity to the gospel. The increase of reactionary organizations within the Protestant and Catholic churches has resulted in a sharp turn toward a hard, sectarian, and exclusive Christianity.

Although evangelical Protestants have traditionally shown hostility toward the "papist" church, the past quarter-century has seen the formation of coalitions of right-wing organizations in Catholic and Protestant churches, based on their common hostility toward the advancement of women's equality and gay rights. Protestant and Catholic fundamentalists are dedicated to the enforcement of the truth "from above" by means of power. Though the followers of these two branches of Christianity approach their truths from the paths of different traditions, they have recently arrived at a remarkably similar destination, sharing many elements of a common analysis about the state of the world and the remedy for its ills. Protestant fundamentalists find their truth in a literal interpretation of a selected number of passages in the Bible. For Catholic fundamentalists, it is a selected number of papal teachings that are endowed with quasi-divine authority.

Both share the view that life for Christians was better in the past, before modern secular democracies began the process of separating church and state. Previously held certainties about Christian morality, especially sexual ethics, are, they hold, compromised in a modern democratic state which insists that the state should protect a diversity of beliefs and lifestyles and the right to freedom of conscience. American evangelicals hark back to what they view as a golden age of Puritan theocracy in the Massachusetts Bay Colony, when the power of the state was at the disposal of the church. Catholic reactionaries look back to a pre–Vatican II age of papal power, when Catholics were united and obedient, every statement of the pope was invested with the aura of infallibility, and states where Catholicism was the religion of the majority could enforce Catholic morality on all citizens.

There is a certain attraction in the appeal for a return to a homogeneous Christian identity. It provides an emotional and spiritual refuge for many who are confused by what appears to be an increasingly chaotic and hostile postmodern world. But right-wing Christian churches provide more than a haven for hurt souls. In the past twenty-five years, fundamentalists have come out of the closet in order to campaign aggressively against the tolerance and inclusiveness of the modern, secular, and democratic state. For the born-again believer, tolerance of a variety of beliefs by the state is tantamount to enforcing a godless relativism. The postmodern liberal democratic state represents a betrayal of the Christian civilization to which Europe and North America owe their origins.

They fail to see the historical irony in this position. Democracy, human rights, the equality of men and women, and the right of all to participate equally in the stewardship of the earth has ancient biblical roots as far back as the creation of humanity in the likeness of God recounted in the Book of Genesis. Jesus announced the good news that all are to participate without discrimination in the kindom and community of God. But the tolerance and inclusiveness of the democratic societies of Europe and North America were achieved only after a long, often bloody struggle with the forces of autocracy and reaction, represented by kings and nobility, whose divine right to rule was supported by the churches. Christian churches, both Catholic and Protestant, have, with few exceptions, fiercely opposed the historical advancement of democratic values and civil rights for women and minorities. It has been the democratic secular state, sometimes enlightened by individual Christian visionaries such as Martin Luther King Jr., that has enshrined the biblical ideal of equality and justice within its civil codes. And it is also only as a result of the protection of freedom of speech and conscience enshrined within the laws of democratic societies that Christians today have the right to promote their values within society at large.

But right-wing Christians have not reconciled themselves with modern, pluralistic, secular society that honors the human rights of all without discrimination. It irks them to have to accept that all citizens, including gays and lesbians for example, are entitled to justice, freedom of speech, and the right to engage in meaningful work and fulfilling relationships. Christians of many denominations have entered the political arena in order to infuse their version of exclusive and intolerant Christian values into public civil discourse. Evangelical churches have now been joined by Catholic groups in pursuit of an aggressive politics of confrontation with the democratic secular world. There is now a real danger that conservative religious groups, under the guise of what they define as "religious freedom," will make demands on the state to restrict the equal rights of all citizens. Although the Catholic Church does not allow democracy or freedom of speech within its own structure, Catholic bishops and priests use the democratic rights of free speech afforded them within secular society to preach intolerance toward the advancement of gay rights, for example, in the public sphere. The civil liberties of all citizens, locally and internationally, are threatened by the current attempt by religious groups to recolonize the public sphere. This is increasingly the case in countries, such as the United States, where politicians actively seek endorsement and legitimacy from religious groups.

THE IDEOLOGIES of Catholic and Protestant reactionary groups have converged today under the umbrella of what are loosely called "family values." According to this set of tenets, there is but one normative version of family, and that is the patriarchal, heterosexual one. "Family values" means deference to male headship, enforced heterosexuality, control of women's sexuality and reproductive options, and the physical disciplining of children. Women fulfill their God-given destiny in the family by being childbearers and homemakers, while men rule the private and public domains inside and outside the home. Proponents of family values also embrace uncritically the consumer lifestyle enjoyed in more affluent parts of the world, where the rich reap the advantages of cheap sweatshop labor of families in underdeveloped nations. They also contend that humans have a God-given right to dominate the earth by continuing, for example, to extract fossil fuels and to maintain clear-cut logging regardless of the damage to the natural environment.[2]

Right-wing Christian apologists view the neoconservative economics of competition, support of the free market system, and the privatization of all health care, housing, and education as consonant with Christian values. The past twenty years have witnessed a close alliance between the religious right and business leaders, who are often recruited through corporate-sponsored events such as prayer breakfasts. The spiritual input at these gatherings stresses personal spirituality, morality, and family values, but does not touch on the social ethics of business or consumption. Anything that is remotely

related to socialism, such as social assistance and government funding of housing and health care, is viewed as tainted with communism
and therefore, by inference, atheism. Their positions betray a curi-
ously contradictory approach to state intervention. They insist that
the state intervene in the private lives of all citizens to promote only
their right-wing version of private family values, but they are opposed
to any state regulation of the economy or the market. The Catholic
Church has developed a body of theoretical teaching on social justice
that supports a notion that the state exists to guarantee the "common
good" of all citizens. But these days, this teaching languishes on the
back burner of Catholic public discourse and practice.

A strict hierarchy of gender, rigid ideas about the place and role
of women, together with a strict control over human sexuality, form
the core of the "pro-family" and anti-feminist agenda. Control of
women's bodies and lives is central to this. The movement for the revival of male headship in the family in evangelical Protestant churches
has become a partner in the Vatican's international crusade against
feminism. Protestant teaching supports the current papal views on
masculine and feminine roles, which denies the social construction of
gender, and insists on preserving fundamental, God-given differences
between men and women. The heterosexual nuclear family is elevated as the highest exemplar of Christian discipleship. This nuclear
family constitutes a sovereign unit unto itself. No national or international regulation must invade this sovereign domain except insofar
as it enforces the heterosexual, Christian model of family. The United
Nations conferences on women, population, and children that have
been held over the past thirty years have been the target of an aggressive campaign by right-wing Catholic and Protestant "family values"
groups opposed to women's equality and reproductive choice.[3]

The nuclear family, in their view, is also best served within a state
economy organized according to the patriarchal capitalism that is the
preferred model of right-wing Christian economics. This sanctifies the
right to the unfettered enjoyment of wealth and the right to private
property, and limits the government's right to tax private income. It
is not surprising, then, that the Christian right has found a political
home within the U.S. Republican Party. Republican governments led
by Presidents Ronald Reagan and George H. W. Bush saw their political and economic goals achieved by enlisting the Vatican's help in the
dismantling of communism in Eastern Europe. Now under George W.
Bush, Republicans have once more made common cause with Rome

and with evangelical Protestants to combat the global movements of feminism and gay rights which they view as a threat to the patriarchal family and the neoconservative state. A similar movement by anti-choice groups within Canada to promote a socially conservative agenda through the right-wing federal Alliance Party, though, has failed to win over the majority of voters.

A theology that insists on the regulation of family life but is neutral toward the conditions of the workplace has also proved to be a natural partner of the consumer economy, the postcommunist "free" market. But outside the affluent societies of North America and Europe, the majority of workers and their families have been impoverished and dehumanized by the advance of globalization. Within those societies, the gap between rich and poor is increasing at an alarming rate. The new right-wing blocs within the churches have by and large ignored this systemic injustice. Inordinate wealth, a frequent target of Jesus himself, is hardly ever the object of their conservative critique.

THE SUCCESS OF THIS Catholic and Protestant conservative revival owes much to two men: Catholic Cardinal Josef Alois Ratzinger and evangelical Pat Robertson. In the past twenty-five years, both men have shaped the way Catholic and Protestant Christianity has responded to the contemporary world. Although they have traveled by different routes, their journeys have converged at a similar destination. Both men share a common approach to truth: it is to be placed at the service of power. Ratzinger shares with John Paul II the vision of a restored Christendom, Romanized and Catholic. Robertson envisages a new theocracy in America through augmenting the power of the U.S. Christian right within the Republican Party. Ratzinger and Robertson share the view that a return to what they define as traditional Christian values is essential to the survival of Western civilization. Ratzinger shares John Paul II's vision of a revival of Christendom in Western Europe, invigorated with the influence of a re-Christianized Eastern Europe. Likewise, the return of America to what he views as its origins as "One Christian Nation under God" is the driving force of Pat Robertson's Christian Coalition. Robertson recently announced his resignation from the Christian Coalition. Ratzinger is seventy-five, the age designated for retirement of Catholic bishops. But the mark left by these two men will endure in their respective denominations long after their retirement.

Ratzinger and Robertson exhibit a suspicious, often hostile attitude to the contemporary world. They view the defeating of the forces of liberalism and secularism and the ending of the separation of church and state as essential components of their mission. They share a visceral hostility to feminism, homosexuality, and liberation theology, as well as a belief that the way to God is through uncritical obedience to the authority of God's duly anointed representatives. Dissent of any kind weakens the church, and is not to be tolerated.

Ratzinger is an intellectual giant compared to Robertson, but the exercise of his official position as head of the Congregation for the Doctrine of the Faith and guardian of the Faith of the Fathers has led him to promulgate an often simplistic and shallow rendering of Catholic truth, one which violates its rich and diverse tradition. An example of this is the 1994 declaration *Ordinatio Sacerdotalis* on the ordination of women to the priesthood. According to this teaching, because women and men are so fundamentally different, no woman can even symbolically represent Christ at the altar. The headship of the church, like that of the family, must remain in male hands. The declaration also states that the church has never ordained women, and because it has never been done, the church has no authority to do it now or in the future. The topic is now closed. The following year, a clarification issued by Ratzinger's Congregation for the Doctrine of the Faith stated that this teaching forms part of the central truth, or deposit of faith, of the church and therefore commands universal assent. Any discussion of the theological and scriptural complexity of this issue is forbidden in favor of a simple resort to authority. But the attempt to impose an injunction on the discussion of the issue has been a dismal failure.

In June 2001 Catholic women from the WOW movement (Women's Ordination Worldwide) gathered for a conference in Dublin. Messages were sent from Ratzinger's office to the conference speakers notifying them that Rome would not tolerate any public presentations on the topic of women's ordination. Ironically, the only speaker who obeyed Ratzinger was a Protestant, Aruna Gnadadson, the representative from the World Council of Churches, who cancelled her appearance. Two nuns who were scheduled to speak, Sr. Joan Chittister, O.S.B., and Sr. Myra Poole, S.N.D., were threatened with "canonical penalties" including excommunication if they went ahead. Both defied this intimidation and spoke at the conference. An amazing reversal ensued: the Vatican backed down! In a message sent to the two women's superiors the following day, the pope's spokesperson, Joaquín Navarro-Valls, issued a statement that "in this case" there were no plans to proceed with disciplinary measures. This marks an unprecedented acknowledgment by Rome that it is losing control over the minds of the faithful and that its erroneous teaching on women's ordination can no longer be defended.

These women who stood up to the Vatican penetrated the psychological barrier of fear which has often provided an impermeable shield for the Vatican's inflexible assertion of its monopoly of truth. There are good grounds for nuns to be fearful of challenging Rome. Excommunication would mean not only a loss of livelihood within the church but also a ban on the reception of the sacraments until such time as they publicly repent. But in her masterful letter to Ratzinger explaining her reasons for supporting Chittister's decision to speak at the conference, her monastic superior, Sister Christine Vladimiroff, reaches back into an older Catholic tradition of obedience.

"My decision should in no way indicate a lack of communion with the Church," she wrote. "I am trying to remain faithful to the role of the 1500-year-old monastic tradition within the larger Church. We [the Benedictines] trace our tradition to the early Desert Fathers and Mothers of the fourth century who lived on the margins of society in order to be a prayerful and questioning presence to both church and society. Benedictine communities of men and women were never intended to be part of the hierarchical or clerical status of the Church, but to stand apart from this structure and offer a different voice. Only if we do this can we live the gift that we are for the Church. Only in this way can we be faithful to the gift that women have within the Church."[4] This is an obedience that takes the time to listen (as its origin in the Latin word *ob-audire* suggests) to the truth spoken in the depths of a being where the soul and the Spirit meet. It is an obedience that liberates because it is founded on integrity, unlike the false obedience fueled by fear that Sara described in her letter. Sara's false obedience had provided her with a temporary illusion of security but could not be sustained when she began to listen to the movement of the Spirit within her true self. Opus Dei's blind obedience to authority, which Sara ultimately rejected, lacks the authenticity of the true *ob-audire* obedience that is the basis of fidelity to conscience.

The emotional intimidation that is used as a tactic by right-wing groups is the result of a deep-seated fear of accepting women on equal terms. There exists in conservative Christian circles today an inchoate fear that the world of white male heterosexual dominance, on which their version of Christianity is based, is being challenged. Their method of defense is to attempt to stamp out contrary opinions with more dogma, charges of heresy, and the excommunication of dissidents. While Ratzinger and Robertson have differences in background and education, the two major issues on which their views converge are socialism and sex. Although Catholicism has developed a body of clear teaching on social justice, these doctrines have been muted over the past twenty-five years in favor of a preoccupation with private sexual morality. Justice for all, the necessary role of the state in securing the common good of all citizens through the redistribution of wealth by taxation, and governments' duty to provide the basic necessities of life for all citizens are foundational principles of Catholic social doctrine.

There are a number of reasons that Catholic hierarchies have toned down the church's message about social morality. In addition to Pope John Paul II's personal crusade against feminism, U.S. political interests have also played a major role. Shortly after being elected pope, John Paul II forged an alliance with President Ronald Reagan to orchestrate the overthrow of communism first in Poland and then in the rest of Eastern Europe. In return, Reagan exacted a price: the suppression of liberation theology on the U.S.'s doorstep in Latin America.[5]

Anything remotely resembling Marxist ideology was anathema to Ratzinger and John Paul II. Any movement that threatened U.S. hemispheric hegemony was anathema to Reagan. Protestant fundamentalists also saw God's design for Christian America threatened by communist influence from the south. The long-term result has been the opening of Latin America to U.S.-led globalization, and its economic transformation into a privatized market economy where the suffering of the poor has been magnified. Ironically, for the Catholic Church, the crushing of Catholic liberation theology has also opened the way for Protestant evangelicals to make new converts with a version of Christianity that preaches individual, "born-again" salvation in the next world rather than liberation in this world. This is a much better fit with a global free-market economy structured here on earth on the economic exploitation of the poor.

THE CONFLUENCE of Catholicism with capitalism has been a marked trend of the conservative Catholicism which has dominated the second half of John Paul II's pontificate. This has meant that by the beginning of the third millennium, with globalization in full swing, there has been little coherent opposition to it from the Catholic Church, either locally or internationally. The Republican ascendancy and the presidency of George W. Bush have seen the church in the U.S. a willing handmaid in the privatization of state assistance to the poor, the sick, and the unemployed. In order to climb on the bandwagon of Bush's cancellation of contraceptive services overseas and the restriction of sterilization and abortion in hospitals at home, the Catholic bishops have muted the church's unpopular messages on economic justice, the common good, nonviolence, and the duty to care for the poor.

The U.S. episcopate's reaction to the "war on terrorism" reflects a shift to the right and a reversal in the previous trend in Catholic thinking toward acceptance of pacifism and nonviolence that had been growing since World War II and the Vietnam war. In 1983, the U.S. bishops issued a pastoral letter on peace. *The Challenge of Peace: God's Promise and Our Response* questions the validity of the notion of the possibility of a just war in the unprecedented circumstances of a nuclear age. In the last century, two factors have come into play which have called in question the application of the just war theory to any circumstances. One is a more radical reappropriation of the very early tradition of Christian nonviolence under any circumstances. The other is the proliferation of weapons of mass destruction, the effect of which far exceeds any of the criteria laid down for the use of force in the case of a just war. A critical rethinking of the just war theory was reflected in the U.S. bishops' 1983 document.

Ten years later, *The Harvest of Justice Is Sown in Peace* drew back from the brink of condemning all resort to violence in a nuclear age and reaffirmed the teaching on the just war. In this second letter, the bishops call for an analysis of the systemic causes of war as rooted in poverty and injustice and a response which takes into account sustainable development and the economic empowerment of the poor. The response of the U.S. bishops to the war on Afghanistan, launched after the terrorist attack on the World Trade towers and the Pentagon on September 11, 2001, also stresses the need for the U.S. to move toward the elimination of the gap between rich and poor. But the bishops, and the Vatican itself in its official statements in response to the bombings, are cautiously supportive of the bombing of Afghanistan as consonant with the requirements of a just war. As one commentator at the time perceptively remarked: "These statements tend to favor the views of U.S. Republicans, many of whom are Catholic. The party is strongly anti-abortion and favors government aid to Catholic schools."[6]

The rightward turn of the U.S. Catholic episcopate on this and other issues over the past twenty years has aligned the U.S. Catholic Church more closely with Pat Robertson's Christian Coalition. In the 1970s, the Protestant Pro-Family Forum issued a compilation of the beliefs attributed to "secular humanism" that the Pro-Family groups condemn. In addition to the denial of God, the existence of hell, and the biblical account of creation, they identify as anathema[7] for Christians "belief in the removal of distinctive roles of male and female...belief in the equal distribution of America's wealth to reduce poverty and bring about equality, belief in the control of the environment, control of energy and its limitation, and the belief in the removal of American patriotism and the free-enterprise system, disarmament, and the creation of a one-world socialistic government."[8]

AMERICAN PROTESTANT FUNDAMENTALISM is not a new phenomenon, even though it does not have as long a history as Catholic conservatism. Its narrow and nationalistic interpretation of Jesus' message is a distortion of the truth about God's love that Jesus gave his life for. A central element in its platform is the notion that the United States was founded as a Christian nation. "America," said Republican senator Jesse Helms in an address to the Christian Coalition's 1996 Convention, "was born in God's name.... This nation was created in God's name and was intended to be a Christian nation." The first Puritans who settled in the Massachusetts Bay colony in the seventeenth century viewed themselves in religious terms as God's elect, founders of a new Eden or the second city of Jerusalem described in the Book of Revelation. The influence of their Calvinist principles resulted in the organization of a theocratic government that emphasized hellfire and damnation and established a strict separation between saved and unsaved. Although the Calvinist hold over the politics of New England states was eventually broken, a hellfire-and-brimstone type of populist preaching continued to be popular.

The eighteenth century saw the birth of a number of revivalist movements. Preachers emphasized the emotional dimension of conversion as well as the imminence of divine judgment upon sinners.

Mainstream Protestant churches, though, adhered to the tolerance, religious freedom, and separation of church and state that were built in to the Declaration of Independence. But small revivalist cults continued to flourish, their hallmark being the camp or tent meeting. Preachers spelled out the details of damnation with dire warnings of the fire of hell and the necessity for immediate conversion. Many in their audience would respond by shaking and speaking in tongues. The focus was on certain "fundamentals," especially biblical texts that focused on the Second Coming and God's impending judgment upon sinners.

The 1914–18 war was a turning point in their notion of God's imminent judgment upon the world. It appeared that this conflict must herald the final battle of Armageddon depicted in the Book of Revelation, the prelude to God's judgment upon a sinful world. The Germans were not just territorial aggressors; they also represented the modern evils of rationalism and Freudian psychology and literary criticism of the Bible. But the end times did not materialize. Instead, the League of Nations came into being. It was named as the "Antichrist" in evangelical literature, because it was viewed as a step toward the united world government of the "end times" that would come under the sway of Satan. But even the horror of World War II did not unleash the last days, although the Nazi Holocaust was interpreted by evangelicals as the last persecution of the "unbelieving Jews" before the coming of the Reign of Christ. The refounded United Nations was a sign that the kingdom of the Antichrist was entering the last phase of its world domination.

But because the end of the world has not taken place, fundamentalists have been forced into a reassessment of their belief in the final judgment. Postwar evangelicals came up with an explanation for this delay. God's wrath would be constrained and the "end times" would continue to be postponed only if America would return to its original foundation as a Christian nation. In the 1960s a new generation of political activists took center stage in a fight to inveigh against what they viewed as a tide of chaos and moral relativism that had overtaken America. The ideology behind this new political activism is reconstructionism, which seeks to replace democracy with theocracy and to abolish the pluralist, democratically elected, and representative government in favor of a Christian state that would govern according to the fundamentalist version of biblical law. "The Christian goal for the world is the universal development of biblical theocratic republics, in which every area of life is redeemed and placed under the Lordship of Jesus Christ and the rule of God's law."[9]

In 1973, Rousas John Rushdoony, one of the original reconstructionist leaders, published *The Institutes of Biblical Law,* an explanation of the Ten Commandments and their application to today. Rushdoony calls for the death penalty to be administered for, among other things, homosexuality, incorrigible juvenile delinquency, and, in the case of women only, "unchastity before marriage."[10] He endorses unfettered capitalism, a minimal national government, no social services outside of the charity of the churches, and the abolition of the public school system. "Pluralism" writes Gary North, another leader in the movement, "will be shot to pieces in an ideological (and perhaps even literal) crossfire, as Christians and humanists sharpen and harden their positions in 'an escalating religious war.' "[11]

In 1979, the year after John Paul II had been elected pope, Jerry Falwell founded the Moral Majority and fired the opening salvo in the new religious war. In 1980, John Paul appointed Josef Ratzinger as head of the Holy Office. Though it was not apparent at the time, these events were to mark the beginning of a new alliance between two formerly hostile denominations and a new mood of militancy on the Christian right.

Like Karol Wojtyla, Josef Ratzinger was a seminarian when the Nazis came to power in Germany. Though never a member of the Nazi party, Ratzinger did spend a brief period in the Hitler Youth. This firsthand experience with Nazism eventually left him with strong convictions about the role of theology. It must remain within the boundaries of the church, subject to its authority and not mingled with secular thought, otherwise it will be tainted by corrupt ideology, either that of the totalitarian state or of the liberal relativism of modern democracies.[12]

Ratzinger rejects liberation theology's vision, that the reign of God can be anticipated within the structures of the world. His early doctoral work on fourteenth-century theologian St. Bonaventure was influential in the formation of his theology. Ratzinger studied Bonaventure's conflict with the visionary Joachim of Fiore. Joachim of Fiore taught that a third age of history would eventually dawn when, in the words of Mary's Magnificat, the poor would be raised up and the rich removed from their thrones. This would happen in this world rather than the next. Bonaventure rejected the idea that the reign of God could be realized in a concrete context within human history. Likewise, Ratzinger's vision of the mission of the church is that it should consist in providing the means for the salvation of the soul for eternity rather than comforting body and soul in the here and now.

Ratzinger's suspicion of modern culture was intensified when student protests erupted in Europe in 1968. He had returned from the council in 1966 to take up an appointment as professor of theology at the University of Tübingen. Two years later, turmoil erupted within the church when Paul VI issued the encyclical *Humanae Vitae.* Contrary to widespread expectation, the pope did not follow the opinion of the majority of the special commission he had established to examine the church's teaching on birth control. Instead, Paul VI reasserted the traditional condemnation of all forms of birth control except the rhythm method. The widespread defiance of this and the protests within the church seemed to mirror the chaos of the student protests on the streets. To Ratzinger, this was one more sign of the fallacy of *aggiornamento,* a modernization of the church and dialogue with the world, because this would lead church and world into chaos. Hence Ratzinger's rejection of liberation theology and feminism as a politicization of the gospel. He believes that the church exists to evangelize the world, not to enter into a dialogue with culture. Its message cannot be interpretation through the lens of class or gender analysis.

THE HARASSMENT OF CATHOLIC SCHOLARS by Ratzinger and local self-appointed watchdogs of Catholic orthodoxy has continued unabated in the past five years, despite John Paul II's much publicized apology in the year 2000 for the sins of the Inquisition. The attempt to suppress theological pluralism within the Catholic community has been stepped up. Sr. Carmel McEnroy was dismissed from St. Meinrad's Seminary in Indiana in 1995 after she signed a public statement supporting women's ordination. In June 1995, Brazilian theologian Ivone Gebara was silenced and sent for a period of study at a Dominican convent in France. Following a demotion that precluded her from teaching seminarians, Sr. Barbara Fiand resigned from the Athenaeum of Ohio in May 1998 after a distinguished teaching career of seventeen years. In July 1998, Liturgical Press of Collegeville, Minnesota, destroyed all its remaining stock of the book *Woman at the Altar,* by Sr. Lavinia Byrne of Cambridge, England. The Vatican condemned the book several years after it was published. Byrne subsequently resigned from her order, the Institute of the Blessed Virgin Mary, after more than twenty years as a nun. In November 1998, law professor Luigi Lombardi Vallauri was suspended from teaching at Milan's Catholic University of the Sacred Heart for questioning the reality of hell and the extent of papal authority. In July 1999, Sr. Jeannine Gramick and Fr. Bob Nugent were ordered to cease their ministry with homosexuals and ordered to remain silent on the church's teaching on homosexuality and on the process that led to their silencing. Nugent complied. Gramick, after much soul searching, decided not to. Ed and Anne Reynolds, lay eucharistic ministers in Pearl River, New York, for twenty years, were pressured to resign from their ministry in August 1999 after they wrote letters to the local paper in support of Gramick and Nugent. In August 1999, Michael Stoeber, an expert on world religions at the Catholic University of America, was denied tenure on the basis of an essay he had written in 1990, which compared the Hindu doctrine of reincarnation with the resurrection.

In April 2000, Shirley Osterhaus, director of campus ministry at Western Washington University in Bellingham, Washington, for fifteen years, was fired with no due process. The reason for her firing was complaints from a local priest, a conservative appointee in his first year of service after ordination who opposed Osterhaus's use of inclusive language, her welcoming attitude toward gays and lesbians, and her opposition to U.S. economic and political policies in the third world. In May 2000 the University of Nijmegen in Holland was forced by the Vatican to withdraw plans to name a chair in theology after Fr. Edward Schillebeeckx for his eighty-fifth birthday, after conservative Catholics complained about his comments in an interview that the traditional teaching on the divinity of Christ needs to be rephrased. Also in August 2000, Fr. Roger Haight, professor of christology at the Jesuit School of Theology in Weston, Massachusetts, was silenced pending an investigation of his book *Jesus Symbol of God*. In December 2000, the Vatican censured Fr. Reinhard Messner, professor of liturgy at the University of Innsbruck in Austria, for suggesting that later church traditions should be judged in the light of their conformity to primitive Christian experience and tradition. Facing an investigation for a book he edited called *Inquisition and Freedom*, Fr. Paul Collins resigned from the priesthood in Melbourne, Australia, in February 2001.

Ratzinger's Holy Office must take much responsibility for a mean-spirited and dysfunctional culture that has arisen within the church, which has resulted in both petty, as well as high-profile, censorship. Tattling to Rome has become the favorite pastime of zealous local watchdogs of orthodoxy. This tale-telling extends to all levels and stultifies the Spirit in Catholic parishes, schools, colleges, and universities. Ratzinger's empire is based on truth that has become disconnected from reality. But his world, constructed on pure, authoritarian reasoning, is an illusion.

In September 2000, there was a dramatic illustration of the effects of this when the Vatican issued a document that sparked instant, shocked reaction around the world. Entitled *Dominus Jesus (The Lord Jesus)*, the statement, endorsed by both John Paul II and Ratzinger, claimed that Catholicism was the only true religion and the only means of salvation for all of humanity. In an elaboration on the teaching of *Dominus Jesus,* John Paul II stated that "it would be erroneous to consider the Church as a way of salvation equal to those of other religions, which would be complementary to the Church.... Even in their sincere search for the truth they are in fact ordered to Christ and his Body, the Church. Nevertheless, they find themselves in a *deficient situation* compared to those who have the fullness of salvific means in the Church" (emphasis added).[13]

Brazilian theologian Leonardo Boff described the teaching of *Dominus Jesus* thus: "Christ is the telephone, but the only operator is the church. All local and long distance calls must come through the church."[14] He concludes that the document means "any initiative by the Vatican in the area of ecumenism is in reality a farce, or else the laying of the groundwork for a trap." Gregory Baum, a Canadian theologian with more than thirty years of experience working in the field of ecumenism, reacted as follows:

> Vatican II led to an understanding of Christian faith that inspires openness to people of other religions or of no religion at all, an openness that is sensitive to the drama of personal and social transformation taking place in their lives. The new Declaration reaffirms this teaching — not with joy but with fear. Cardinal Ratzinger is afraid that this new openness to transformative religious and secular experience may prompt Catholic theologians, eager to account for religious pluralism in God's world, to relativize Christian faith and regard all religions as true in their own way.[15]

This reemphasis on the unique and exclusive path to salvation provided by the Catholic Church is the latest dimension of the reversal

of the direction of the Second Vatican Council that has been initiated
by Ratzinger.

ANOTHER OF HIS CAMPAIGNS has been a stealth attack on the reforms of the liturgy, which were one of the most striking outcomes
of the council.

First, he has attacked an inclusive language translation of scriptural and liturgical texts. ICEL (International Commission on English
in the Liturgy), which came into being in the wake of the liturgical
reforms of the Second Vatican Council, was set up by the bishops
of the English-speaking world. For the past twenty years it has been
working on and producing translations of liturgical texts for English-
speaking Catholic countries. In a series of moves starting in December
of 1999, Ratzinger's Holy Office has attempted to impose its restorationist agenda on the work of the committee and to wrest control of
it from the hands of local bishops and into the direct supervision of
Rome.[16] In October 1999 Rome moved to assume control of ICEL
by demanding the right to veto staff appointed to the commission.
Although this move was resisted by some bishops, this resistance was
short-lived.[17] In May 2001, the decree *Liturgiam Authenticam* (Authentic liturgy) laid down new rules for the translation and revision
of liturgical texts. It rejects the use of inclusive language as an "overly
servile adherence to prevailing modes of expression" and states that
translations from Latin should be as literal as possible. The Vatican
"will be involved more directly" in the work of translation.

In addition to endorsing the celebration of the liturgy in the language of the people, the Second Vatican Council also initiated a return
to the ancient idea of liturgy as the "work" of the whole People of
God. The role of the priest as the sole conduit of sacramental grace
from God and the only member of the community fit and pure enough
to occupy the sacred space of the sanctuary was downplayed. Lay
women, as well as men, could enter into the sacred space as readers
and ministers of communion. Communion rails — which symbolically marked the boundaries of the priest's sacred space from the body
of the church where the ordinary, unconsecrated faithful watched the
priest perform his sacred rituals from afar — were removed. Priests
began to move out of the sanctuary to preach or to give the sign of
peace before communion, and lay people felt free to step into the
sanctuary and even to gather round the altar.

A decree from Ratzinger's office promulgated by John Paul II in

March 2000 reverses these reforms in favor of a return to a hierarchically ordered and priest-centered eucharistic celebration. The
document starts from the premise that "the eucharistic celebration
touches them [priest and people] in different ways.... Therefore all,
whether ordained ministers or Christian faithful, by virtue of their
function or office, should do all and only those parts which belong
to them."[18] The manner in which these different functions of priests
and people are delineated provides a significant disclosure of the ideology behind Ratzinger's restoration. To read this document is to be
transported back into the 1950s, when the priest was a symbol of
purity of the church that must be guarded by means of separation
from the world. The secular world, as represented by the laity, was
kept in its place, away from the holy vessels or the sanctuary. Now,
once again, no lay minister may approach the altar until after the
priest has received communion. Neither may any lay minister touch
the consecrated hosts to transfer them into multiple vessels for dis-
tributing communion. Only the priest may open the tabernacle to
place leftover consecrated hosts within it. Lay people must never expound on the Word of God by participating in the sermon nor may
they open their mouths to say any of the words of consecration reserved solely for the priest to pronounce. The priest is made a virtual
prisoner in the sanctuary: he must not transgress the boundary separating the anointed ones from the great unwashed mass of the faithful
by entering their part of the church to shake their hands at the sign
of peace.

Such minute delineation of roles, the deliberate separation of what
is set apart, celibate, and therefore purer and more suited to deal with
the transcendent divine than the sexualized bodies of the mass of the
faithful, is an example of Ratzinger's disembodied Platonic idealism
in action. The emphasis on the transcendence of God, on salvation
as consisting in attaining a heavenly realm where holy beings dwell
at one with God, and on the liturgy as being a foretaste of this on
earth is the hallmark of Ratzinger's spirituality and that of the Christian Coalition. His aim is to make the church on earth once again
an unsullied sign of the mystery of God in the world. This other-
worldliness is not framed in Robertson's crudely apocalyptic vision
of salvation as the battle between the armies of Satan and the armies
of the Lord, but it fosters a similar contempt for the concrete realities
and struggles of this world.

In response to widespread criticism of these new liturgical rules, a further document clarifying the reason for the restoration was issued from Ratzinger's office on December 6, 2000. It makes the extraordinary claim that evidence of practices drawn from the earliest sources of Christian tradition cannot be used to critique the actions of church authorities. Ratzinger states that the church does not deduce its certainty on revealed matters solely from the scriptures. Furthermore, "it exceeds the possibilities of theology to explain the word of God in a manner binding for the faith and life of the Church. This duty is entrusted to the magisterium of the Church." All theologians, insists Ratzinger, must teach that Christ instituted each of the seven sacraments (despite incontrovertible evidence that marriage was not incorporated into church teaching as a sacrament until the twelfth century).

This cavalier contempt for the centrality of earliest Christian tradition as a reference point for a reformation of the church today is a reversal of the principles enunciated at Vatican II, which have guided liturgical reform over the past fifty years. Ratzinger's rationale amounts to a kind of fascism reminiscent of the lame arguments advanced by Rome against the ordination of women. Even if the evidence of their minds points to the contrary, Catholics are expected to submit with unquestioning obedience to even the most petty edicts of authority. The lack of trust shown toward priests, the picayune regulations of the movement of priests and people onto and off the altar, small as it may seem in the light of other issues on the world today, are signs of a much deeper realignment of Catholicism that has taken place under Ratzinger and John Paul II. As the ancient Latin aphorism stated: *lex orandi, lex credendi,* which roughly translated means the way people pray signifies what they believe. Ratzinger's restorationist liturgical reforms, as well as his denunciation of the dangers of the ecumenical movement, are an indication of control by power instead of by truth.

THIS PURSUIT OF POWER as a means of mass control is common to Ratzinger and Robertson. Is their version of the role of the Christian community in relation to the rest of the world consonant with what Jesus himself practiced? Robertson's Jesus supports the moralistic and adversarial politics of the religious right. This Jesus is the obedient Son of the strict parent, a moralist on sexual issues and an authoritarian type of "Lord" who wreaks vengeance on all who refuse to follow His way. A distorted image of Jesus as wrathful judge is also used to instill fear and hatred toward those who are different. This is a perversion of the truth of the gospel. But it has proved to be an appealing "quick fix" spiritual solution for many conservative followers of both branches of Christianity. Ratzinger's Jesus is judgmental and enacts a price for nonconformity through the judgments of the magisterium. Ratzinger's Jesus has placed the power to judge, and to excommunicate, firmly in the hands of his representatives on earth, the pope and the bishops. Ratzinger's and Robertson's rationale for their power to visit God's judgment upon dissenters and to promulgate their respective versions of right living on society may be different, but the end result is the same.

The potential political clout that would result from a coalition of right-wing Catholics and evangelical Protestants has not been lost on protagonists from both sides. "We are one" declared Pat Robertson after meeting with the late Cardinal John O'Connor of New York. Cardinal O'Connor responded: "I believe that the evangelicals and Catholics in America, if they work together, can see many pro-family initiatives in our society, and we can also be an effective counterbalance to some of the radical, leftist initiatives, the gay rights and the pro-choice and many other radical groups that are seeking to disrupt and destroy the family values of America."[19]

Several militant groups have indeed arisen within the Catholic Church in response to papal and episcopal calls for a counterbalance to feminism and gay rights in society. They have placed a militant, sectarian face on contemporary Catholicism and forged alliances with the evangelical Protestant movements sparked by Robertson and Falwell. Whereas in the 1960s and 1970s, parents might worry about their children being attracted to groups such as the Moonies or the Hare Krishnas, now it is conservative Christian cults that are a cause for concern.

A cult is an exclusive group. Its members are encouraged to sever normal family connections and give their loyalty to the founder or leader. It claims to have a monopoly on truth. It is voluntary in that an individual chooses to become a member, but once enrolled, it is hard for a person to leave and risk being shunned. The cult demands total and unquestioning allegiance. It promises its members automatic access to their reward in heaven if they follow the founder's rules and threatens eternal damnation if they don't. "Nonbelievers are rejected by God and thus in some inexplicable way are only tentatively human. As such, nonbelievers are dispensable. If they intrude in the believers' world the psychological conditions exist to make it possible for believers to accommodate violence toward nonbelievers."[20]

Extremist anti-abortion groups, such as the Army of God and the Lambs of Christ, provide hit lists of abortion providers on their websites as the objects of their Christian *jihad*.[21] This is the frightening face of religious fundamentalism, Protestant and Catholic, and its newly found militancy.

In the letter from Sara quoted at the beginning of this chapter, she mentioned that most of her friends had joined Opus Dei, a Catholic version of the Moral Majority. Opus Dei, or the Work of God, was founded in Spain in 1928 by Josemaría Escrivá. It initially drew members from the military and business classes in Spain. Opus Dei threw its support behind dictator Francisco Franco's cause in the Spanish Civil War and formed its own brigade to fight against the communists. The influence of the movement in Spain continues. Spain's economic resurgence within the European Community is seen by some Opus members in Spain as an opportunity to re-create that new Catholic Crusade in Western Europe so dear to the heart of John Paul II.[22]

A renewed emphasis on lay spirituality was a central aspect of the engagement of the church with the modern world envisaged by the Second Vatican Council. But the council's appreciation for the strengths and goodness of the modern world was not welcomed by traditionalists such as Escrivá. The new spirituality envisaged by the council called for an acceptance of the world on its own terms, conscious of the fact that Christians had not always been right and must make atonement for past sins. Catholic lay people were encouraged to look for signs of the Spirit of God operating outside the church and to work to further this work alongside all people of good will on equal terms. The suspicion, sometimes outright condemnation, with which the church had greeted the birth of modern secular movements such as democracy and feminism was to be set aside in favor of an attempt to find a common ground where the reign of God could be advanced through common works of charity and justice.

Opus Dei, in contrast, has remained locked in a pre–Vatican II perspective of hostility to the world. Opus Dei members are encouraged to go out into the world to sanctify the world, but their communication with society is to be one-way only. They are to be in the world not to learn from it, but to infiltrate it and convert it to the truth. This goes back to a previous concept of mission and evangelization that treats the world as an alien object to be acted upon from a position of superiority, not one of reciprocity or solidarity. Escrivá "had such great animosity toward the Council that he seriously considered leaving the Catholic Church to join the Greek Orthodox Church. He suffered from deep post-conciliar depression."[23] He was vigorously opposed to John XXIII's call for *aggiornamento*, which he viewed as a sign of weakness, one open to the danger of relativism. Truth for him was unchanging not only at its core but also in the peripheral ways in which it is to be transmitted.

DESPITE THE FACT that it promotes itself as a lay organization, Opus Dei is dominated by priests, members of the Society of the Holy Cross. As of now there are thought to be about two thousand Opus Dei priests. The organization of Opus Dei is also hierarchical and class-ridden. About 20 percent of the membership consists of "numeraries," who constitute the highest class of full members who undertake perpetual chastity and a promise of unquestioning obedience. They live in gender-segregated communities. The stores where its members may shop for clothes are graded according to status.[24] The male numeraries are encouraged to dress for success and buy their clothes at top-flight establishments. They work in professional fields and donate their salaries to the organization in return for a stipend. The majority of the members of Opus Dei are married, and fall into a lesser category of supernumeraries, the fact that they are married rendering them inferior to the numeraries.

Opus Dei members attend Mass and recite the rosary every day. Practices of physical mortification, the wearing of a spiked metal band, the *cilice,* around the arm or thigh and self-administered whippings with a spiked cord, long abandoned by other religious groups as psychologically suspect, are still practiced. Members must report weekly to a director (some of whom are in their early twenties) and disclose to him all their personal and political activities. All incoming and outgoing mail is read by the director. Confession once a week to an Opus Dei priest is compulsory. Sexual problems and inclinations are a frequent topic of scrutiny.[25] The advice given to Sara by an Opus Dei priest, that she should stay in an abusive relationship and offer it up, reflects a view of one more concerned with the preservation of the status of the group than the psychological and spiritual health of individual members. The sacred seal of confession is treated in a cavalier fashion when it affects the image of the organization. A priest who left Opus Dei recounts that he was berated for not revealing to

his superiors the sin of homosexuality confessed to him by a peni-
tent. He was told that he should have withheld absolution until the
person involved had disclosed this to a director, who could then use
this information more openly than a confessor. Some time before the
founding of Opus Dei, these practices of intimate disclosure were
recognized as so open to abuse that they were banned in Canon 530
of the 1917 Code of Canon Law,[26] but they are still endorsed by
Opus Dei.[27]

Escrivá left explicit instructions to "conceal the number of members from outsiders."[28] All members are to be aggressive in recruiting
others, concealing from them in the process the hierarchical organization, the celibacy, the disclosure of conscience to the spiritual
director, and the secrecy. "A holy coercion is necessary," wrote Escrivá. " Compelle intrare!' the Lord tells us. You must kill yourselves
for proselytism."[29] The secrecy with which Opus Dei shrouds its
membership and its activities serves to fuel the suspicion that it must
have something to hide. Why, in contradiction to Jesus' message, does
the group hide its light under a bushel? The fact that its members
seem not to be proud of their allegiance raises significant questions.
What possible activities could a Catholic group be indulging in that it
cannot proclaim them from the rooftops? And why should an organization so highly favored by the Vatican find it necessary to operate
under cover of darkness?

Opus Dei's hierarchical organization discriminates against women,
who cannot hold high office within the group. Escrivá never concealed his contempt for women, and for the movement for women's
rights, which he referred to as "synonymous with injustice." Escrivá's former personal assistant, Maria del Carmen Tapia, states that:
"More than once Escrivá remarked about women's lack of sincerity and complained about how complicated they are.... He used to
tell us that he had not wanted women in Opus Dei: 'I didn't want
women in the work. You can truly say it was from God!' "[30] Women
are employed as secretaries, cooks, and cleaners in the male, as well
as female, residences. Male members of Opus Dei are not assigned to
domestic duties.

"Women don't need to be scholars," stated Escrivá in Opus Dei's
journal, *El Camino.* "It is enough for them to be prudent." There
are segregated workshops at conferences specifically for Opus Dei
women on, for example, deportment, "Christian fashion," and mod-
esty. There are no equivalent instructions for men on how to dress

modestly. Women are instructed to purchase their "modest" clothes from cheap chain stores. Like their founder, Opus Dei members still evidently regard women as a source of temptation and a cause of their own misfortune if they lead men astray. It is hard to believe that such attitudes still prevail in a relatively progressive society such as Canada, but Sara's unfortunate experience speaks volumes about the thinly veiled misogyny cultivated by some of the young men who are attracted to Opus Dei. Another Opus Dei spokesperson recently blamed women for causing sexual harassment in the workplace "by going around dressed in such a manner as to invite that approach."[31]

A bizarre remark about sexuality was made by Escrivá's successor, Bishop Javier Echeverría Rodríguez while speaking at a conference organized by Opus Dei in Catania, Sicily, in April 1997. Exhorting his audience to "arrive at marriage with a clean body," Echeverría then linked premarital sex with physical disability, asserting: "A poll states that 90 percent of the handicapped are children of parents who did not come to marriage in purity." In reaction to the storm of protest that his remark elicited from organizations that support the handicapped, Echeverría responded in a letter to the newspaper *Il Messagero* that he was merely trying to illustrate the potentially negative consequences of sexual promiscuity.[32]

Opus Dei seeks to infiltrate the higher echelons of secular institutions and follows a deliberate policy of recruiting members in the political, academic, and medical intelligentsia, in an avowed goal to "hallow and christianize the institutions of the peoples, of science, culture, civilization, politics, the arts and social relations."[33] Opus Dei's aims coincide well with John Paul II's vision of re-creating Christendom in Europe and reviving the traditional sway of the church over politics in Latin America, which has been undermined by liberation theology. Its members have also been willing agents in propagating the papal message against birth control in the underdeveloped world, often distorting the truth to serve this agenda. One example of this is the rhetoric which casts family planning programs in poorer countries as a front for a new "neocolonialism" of the West toward the developing world.[34]

In 1982, John Paul II gave Opus Dei the status of personal prelature. This means that it bypasses the authority of the local bishop and comes directly under the protection of the pope. It is thus immune from enquiry or interference from bishops who might be concerned about negative aspects of its influence. Opus Dei's university in Rome has the status of a Pontifical Institute, whereby it is assured of the pope's personal approval of its curriculum. Opus Dei regards itself as the only group within the church which possesses the fullness of Catholic truth, uncorrupted by interface or dialogue with the world. According to Escrivá: "We are the remnant of the people of Israel. We are the only ones who, having remained faithful to God, can still save the Church today. Given the state of the Church today, it seems as if it were abandoned by the Holy Spirit. We are the ones who can save the Church by our faithfulness to the Father."[35] "Opus Dei responds to John Paul's yearnings for 'the perfect society' (a phrase he often uses) of the Middle Ages, when church and state were inseparable and the church was the only source of salvation.... Such a system has held considerable appeal for the Catholic Church, which has lost much of its earlier power through the rise of labor movements and political parties that espouse socialism and democratic egalitarianism."[36]

Opus Dei now has its first cardinal, Juan Luis Cipriani of Lima, Peru, who was appointed in February 2001. Cipriani has been a vocal supporter of the military in Peru. He has acquired a reputation as an opponent of human rights groups, which he described as "just covering the tails of Marxist and Maoist political movements."[37] Cipriani defended the actions of the military in carrying out a massacre in the village of Cayara, located within his diocese, as a necessary means of extracting information for the government. He shares this admiration for the military with another Opus Dei member of the Latin American hierarchy, Archbishop Saenz Lacalle of San Salvador. In 1997, Saenz Lacalle, the successor of the martyred Archbishop Oscar Romero, accepted the honorary title of brigadier general, a rank he proudly displays alongside colleagues who were directly or indirectly implicated in the assassination of Romero. Such cynicism is an indication of the lengths to which truth has been sacrificed in the service of power.

In the fall of 2002, Josemaría Escrivá de Balaguer will be canonized as a saint. His life will be held up to the Catholic faithful everywhere as an example of heroic and outstanding holiness. Escrivá was beatified, the first step toward canonization, in May 1992. On December 20, 2001, the date when the Vatican announced Escrivá's forthcoming sainthood, Cardinal Jose Saraiva Martins, prefect of the Vatican Congregation for the Causes of Saints, described him as "an eminent figure of the Church of the 20th century, who promoted lay sanctity with tireless fervor and with many initiatives took the leaven of the Gospel to the society of our time."[38]

O PUS DEI'S AMBITION to create a new Christendom extends from Europe and Latin America to the U.S. and Canada. FBI Director Louis Freeh is a supernumerary member of Opus Dei. In February 2001 the exposure of double agent Robert Hanssen focused the attention of the world on Opus Dei. Hanssen was caught by FBI agents as he dropped off a package for an agent in the SVR, the successor of the KGB in the Soviet Union's intelligence network. Interviews and court documents reveal a man who was leading a double, if not a triple, life.

Hanssen, an adult convert to Catholicism, has been a member of Opus Dei since 1978. He became a double agent shortly after this and continued selling secrets to the Russians over a period of fifteen years. Apparently he repeatedly confessed his spying to Opus Dei priests, but the only advice they gave him was to keep praying about it. He struggled with an addiction to pornography and formed a friendship with a stripper, Priscilla Galey. Hanssen told Galey she would go to hell unless she confessed and changed her life. Other friends reported that Hanssen was obsessed with religion, would leave work early to attend anti-abortion rallies, and was constantly trying to get them to join Opus Dei.[39] Although Hanssen's life as a double agent cannot be directly attributed to his membership in Opus Dei, it is troubling that its leaders knew of his activities and did not point out that they were incompatible with Christian principles, nor did they advise him to seek help to deal with his sexual obsessions.

Authoritarian groups such as Opus Dei render people powerless to discern the truth within their daily experience, unmediated by a father figure. This prevents Catholic adults from developing a mature faith, one that is open to the complexity and ambiguity of life. As a result, they remain fearful of change and lacking in trust of God. There is little evidence of a trust in the Holy Spirit to guide the church forward into the new millennium.

As Gil Bailie states, "The myths and rituals of an intact culture do not answer questions; they extinguish the will to ask them. Once a mythological system fails to eliminate such questions, it can never make up for that failure by being logically persuasive.... When a myth fails to extinguish the will to question, the more brilliant the reasoning offered by its defenders, the more the sophisticated reasoning destroys mythological consciousness."[40] Groups such as Opus Dei provide their followers with the comfort of the unchanging symbols and mythology of traditional Catholicism. The rapid spread of liberation theology in several countries in Latin America and its vision of a church "from below" without the trappings of power and the traditional alliance with conservative political parties was a threat to the privileged Catholic classes on that continent. It is from among these groups that Opus Dei has attracted many recruits. Conservative politicians have found willing allies in the business and professional recruits of Opus Dei. And there has been no Romero to speak up for the poor from within the hierarchy.

In 1997, a Belgian parliamentary commission placed Opus Dei on a list of dangerous religious sects. ODAN, the Opus Dei Awareness Network, which was established to provide education, outreach, and support to those adversely impacted by Opus Dei, lists the following as matters for concern about Opus Dei: its aggressive recruitment using teams and staged activities, its recruitment through the use of front groups which do not reveal their true purpose, and the fact that members must report regularly on their own recruiting efforts. The lack of informed consent is also a cause for concern as are some controls — such as opening personal mail, corporal mortification, and the donation of one's entire salary — that are not revealed until after the initial commitment has been made. Members are discouraged from telling their parents about their membership, and the display of pictures of loved ones is discouraged. They are told that if they leave Opus Dei, they will never again enjoy God's approval. When they die they may be damned to hell and thus to an eternity without God.[41]

In 1981, the late Cardinal Hume of Westminster became so disturbed at reports of Opus Dei "fishing" activities among young Catholics that he issued a series of recommendations to be implemented in the diocese of Westminster. This was before his episcopal authority over Opus Dei within his diocese was removed by Pope John Paul's assumption of personal authority over the movement in 1982. No person under the age of eighteen, Hume recommended, was to make a commitment to Opus Dei. Potential recruits should discuss the matter fully with their parents. Individuals should be free to leave the organization without pressure. And Opus Dei must undertake full disclosure of their activities within the diocese. Such disclosure has not been forthcoming in Westminster or elsewhere in the world.

Youth of high school and college age, particularly those who show intellectual aptitude, are often recruited by invitation to parties at clubs or centers which Opus Dei runs in upscale neighborhoods or on university campuses. The name of Opus Dei does not appear nor is there any overt reference to the group. They are then targeted by certain individuals who are already members of Opus Dei and who will eventually become their spiritual directors. Opus Dei recruiters are especially active during World Youth Days.

Potential Opus Dei recruits, for example, are not told about ascetic practices such as self-flagellation until after they have made a commitment to the group; neither are they advised of the necessity of exposing the secrets of their conscience to the spiritual director. They are advised to tell all to him. "In the confidence of younger brothers, all their little secrets and worries of all kinds. In the beginning it is difficult for them. Afterward they come to need it."[42] They are told not to tell their parents about their involvement in Opus Dei until after they have made a commitment to the group. From then on, their attendance at family events such as baptisms or weddings is discouraged.[43]

THE ACTIVITIES of another of John Paul II's favored groups recently came under investigation by Revenue Canada (the Canadian equivalent of the U.S. Internal Revenue Service), which has revoked its charitable status. Human Life International, or HLI, an outgrowth of the Human Life Center at St. John's University in Collegeville, Minnesota, was founded by Benedictine Fr. Paul Marx in 1972. Marx was teaching the rhythm method of birth control to married couples and writing against contraception and abortion. He was ousted from St. John's University in 1980 on account of his extremist and racist views. But in 1981, with encouragement from the Vatican, Marx founded Human Life International. The same year, the Vatican established its Pontifical Council on the Family to coordinate opposition to contraception, abortion, and homosexuality. Another organization that provided HLI's first offices and funding was the Washington-based Free Congress Foundation, a right-wing think tank that was also instrumental in founding Jerry Falwell's Moral Majority.

HLI is now an international organization with some eighty-nine branches in fifty-six countries. It is opposed to contraception, abortion, sex education, feminism, the United Nations, daycare, and gay rights. But there is a strange inconsistency in HLI views. On the one hand, by outlawing contraception and abortion they seek to maintain a high level of population increase, yet they see the large families of nonwhite races as a threat to America's Christian civilization. "I guess we have 250,000 Vietnamese here already," wrote Paul Marx in an HLI publication, "and they are going to have large families; the Orientals always do. God knows how many Mexicans cross the borders every night . . . and if we have to fight the Russians, I wonder if these people will be willing to stake their lives."[44] It is hard to see anything but a racist motivation in this kind of statement. Marx also expressed his concerns about the ending of apartheid in South Africa. He stated in 1990 that the goal of one vote one person would be a disaster because "it is difficult . . . to get tribal peoples one step away from the bush and huts to manage a modern economy and to rule themselves peaceably and democratically."[45]

An undercurrent of anti-Semitism is also evident in Marx's writings. In his autobiography, *Confessions of a Pro-Life Missionary,* Paul Marx devotes a chapter to "Pro-abortion Jews and the New Life Holocaust." Abortion, he argues, is a product of "the same Jewish community that accuses the pope of insensitivity to the Jewish Holocaust but now not only condones but has more or less led the greatest holocaust of all time, the war on unborn babies."[46] "Pro-abortion Jews," he adds, "are prominent among TV/radio/movie executives, authors, columnist etc. . . . Among the chief crusaders for abortion in England, too, were prominent Jews."[47]

Randall Terry, the founder of the U.S. group Operation Rescue, is a frequent speaker at HLI conferences. Terry is a reconstructionist. He believes that before Jesus Christ comes back to set up his kingdom and reign on earth, the churches must first establish the reign of Christ over secular society. Terry's long association with HLI is another example of the convergence of Catholic and Protestant fundamentalism. Terry believes that democracy is a heresy and that biblical law must be imposed on society. At the HLI conference in California in 1994, Terry stated that "we need to preach the law and we need to say unashamedly that our goal is a Christian nation. . . . We can't have it both ways: either God has called us to extend His law over all the earth or he hasn't."[48] This vision of the reign of God includes a return to biblical patriarchy, or the divinely sanctioned headship of the male gender, and the criminalization of homosexuality. It is a vision shared by many on the Catholic right.

The reign of God envisaged by Terry is not one of love, but of hate. "Let a wave of intolerance wash over you," he told a church group in Indiana in 1993. I want you to let a wave of hatred wash over you. Yes, hate is good."[49] The particular targets of Terry's hate are abortion providers. "We've found the weak link is the doctor.... We're going to expose them. We're going to humiliate them." The Christian right takes every opportunity to expose the fact that many of these doctors are Jewish. Terry also holds views derived from a division of reconstructionism known as Christian Identity. The Anglo-Saxon people who colonized the United States are the inheritors of the ten lost tribes of Israel and of the biblical covenant forfeited by the Jews because they did not recognize Christ as the Messiah. Only white males, therefore, will hold authority in the new theocratic state. This theology "informs much of the white supremacist movement in the United States — from the Aryan Nations to the Posse Comitatus."[50]

Another HLI supporter often featured on their website is Don Treshman, who was one of the defendants successfully sued in 1999 for maintaining the website known as the Nuremberg Files, which posted the names and private addresses of abortion providers.[51] In a TV interview broadcast after the shooting of Dr. Garson Romalis, a Vancouver doctor who provided abortion services, Treshman stated "that sniper shooting was certainly the superb tactic. It was certainly far better than anything we've seen in the States because the shooting was done in such a way that the perpetrator got away. I think that more abortionists would quit as a result of that."[52]

In recent years, HLI has suffered setbacks as a result of internal dissent and power struggles. Fr. Paul Marx retired from HLI in 1999, ostensibly for reasons of health. Marx, however, denied that his retirement was voluntary and called his retirement a "coup" engineered by Fr. Richard Welch, C.Ss.R., the president of HLI.[53] It appears that HLI had for some time been experiencing cash flow shortages from mismanagement, abuse of funds by senior staff, and "very bad, un-Christian relationships with employees."[54] A separate group called Donor Rights was established by some HLI staff to protect the contributions of nonemployees and call the board of directors to accountability.

In 1994, Revenue Canada revoked the charitable status of HLI on the grounds that HLI was a political advocacy group and was not devoting the bulk of the funds it raised to charitable activities. Initial concern surfaced at the Ministry of National Revenue in 1989 when HLI sent postcards depicting twenty-week-old aborted fetuses to all members of the Canadian Parliament. HLI was warned in 1993 that its materials and activities did not fall within the parameters of the advancement of education or benefit to the community as defined by Revenue Canada for tax-exempt charitable status. The department cited "publications such as 'The American Holocaust' and 'HLI promoting its own interpretation of controversial issues such as sex education in schools, homosexuality, universal day care, ... overpopulation and the 'new age' movement." They also cited the fact that "HLI's positions go well beyond what is beneficial to the community" and that its publications discouraged support for community organizations such as UNICEF and the United Way.[55]

HLI sought, but failed to obtain, representative status with the Economic and Social Council (ECOSOC) at the United Nations, largely because of the anti-Semitism and outspoken hostility toward the UN itself found in HLI literature. As a result, in 1997 a new organization, CAFHRI (The Catholic Family and Human Rights Institute) was formed under the auspices of HLI Canada. The mandate of the new group, as indicated in the job description of Ann Noonan, the first director of CAFHRI (now also known as C-FAM), was to report directly to HLI Canada, to coordinate with HLI Canada, and to clear media releases through HLI's Canadian office.[56] This group also works closely with the Holy See at the UN. "Holy See requests take priority" states the minutes of C-FAM's first meeting, but the group is to "be discrete [*sic*] about Holy See connection."[57] After only two months, Ann Noonan was replaced as director by Austin Ruse. In a speech shortly afterward, Ruse boasted, "And then we broke every single rule of UN lobbying...."[58]

Because the UN has never had to contend before with groups that participate in the organization with the intent to undermine it from within, it lacks clear guidelines on accreditation and registration for conferences. As a result, C-FAM and other right-wing groups have been able to pack with hostile delegates selective conferences that they target, those concerned with the rights of women and children. By means of various tactics such as swarming, loud vocal disruption, or praying out loud, they intimidate delegates and curtail or impede the work of UN committees. "This time," said Austin Ruse, referring to the Beijing+5 prep-com, "we took over what's known as the Youth Caucus.... We had probably sixty kids, and they went in and took the meeting over."[59] Since the UN works by consensus, it is relatively easy for conservative strategists, acting in concert with conservative states such as the Holy See and its anti-feminist Muslim allies in states such as Sudan and Iran, to block international consensus on issues they oppose. According to Austin Ruse, since the UN works primarily by consensus "a dozen states can stop anything."[60]

The UN also remains a favorite target of Protestant evangelicals, especially since the collapse of communism. Pat Robertson has asserted that the UN is a tool of a secret underground movement of anti-Christian forces that are covertly operating under UN auspices to manipulate the world economy and undermine U.S. national sovereignty in the name of a new world government. This one world government will fall under the sway of the Antichrist and spark the final battle of Armageddon, which will see UN troops hiding in national parks in the United States.[61] U.S. presidents, such as Jimmy Carter and Bill Clinton, who, in Robertson's words, "want a larger community of nations living at peace in our world, are in reality unknowingly and unwittingly carrying out the mission and mouthing the phrases of a tightly knit cabal whose goal is nothing less than a new order for the human race under the domination of Lucifer and his followers."[62]

It is only in recent years that the UN has become the focus of reactionary religious groups. Recent UN conferences, particularly those on women, population, and the environment, have witnessed the birth of a cynical alliance between Catholic and Protestant reactionaries. Using similar stealth tactics to those that proved so successful in infiltrating the Republican Party, they have registered hundreds of members in bogus Non-Governmental Organizations, dedicated to abusing the open and democratic access within the UN in order to undermine the organization from within. Prior to the conferences in the 1990s, Protestant fundamentalists had criticized the UN at home and had influenced the U.S. Congress to cut funds to the United Nations. Why the dramatic shift to a more aggressive strategy? Because in the 1990s, the UN embarked on a series of conferences which set out to analyze and transform the foundations of sexism and gender inequality which form the bedrock of fundamentalist Catholic and Protestant views of the patriarchal family. As a result of some recent progress at the UN in the advancement of women's and children's rights, racial equality, and environmental consciousness (regarded by Christian fundamentalists as a sign of pagan, New Age influence), the past decade has seen a surge of interest in the UN among conservative Christians and an increasing presence of right-wing religious NGOs. Their aim is to put pressure on governments and on the UN itself in order to halt progress toward the universal acceptance of women's rights and to discredit the UN and undermine its influence.

The Population Research Institute (PRI), founded by Paul Marx of HLI in 1989, has attempted to lend scientific credibility to religious groups opposed to the UN's work of extending reproductive rights and dismantling social and cultural barriers to women's equality. A recent PRI Weekly News Briefing attacked the UN for "zealous promotion of population control, radical feminism and the like" that has "sent European populations crashing instead of enacting pro-family, pro-natal policies to increase their birth rates."[63] This attack on the UN disguises the subtle racism that laments the decline of European and U.S. birth rates as a threat to the survival of Christian civilization that is found in much of the literature of the Christian right.

Racist sentiments about the threats to European Christendom are also being aired by members of the Catholic hierarchy. Cardinal Giacomo Biffi is the archbishop of Bologna and considered by some a potential successor to John Paul II. In a pastoral letter of September 13, 2000, Biffi sounded the alarm over the number of new immigrants settling in Italy. "The criteria for admitting immigrants," he wrote, "cannot be only economic. It is necessary that one concern oneself with saving the identity of the nation." Biffi continues to identify the identity of the nation, Italy, with Christianity and to lament the fact that a large proportion of immigrants to Italy are from Muslim countries. Italy's immigration policies, in his view, should favor Catholics.[64] Biffi's remarks drew severe criticism from politicians and some Catholic bishops but garnered support from the Vatican's secretary of state, Cardinal Angelo Sodano. Unabashed, Biffi reiterated his concerns at a recent Catholic Church–sponsored conference on multiculturalism. He stated that the careful selection of Christian immigrants was necessary to avoid a future of "tears and blood." In the same speech, Biffi also called in question the whole idea of dialogue with other religions as "ambiguous to the point of being potentially deviant and alienating" and criticized Pope Paul VI for launching the process without sufficient theological foundation.[65]

Just as Biffi regards immigration from non-Christian countries as a threat to Christian hegemony in Europe, so the Christian right in the U.S. regards the UN as a potentially subversive form of world government which threatens U.S. hegemony and blocks the unfettered global exercise of U.S. strategic self-interest. Right-wing groups also fear that the domestic gains they hope to achieve, such as the repeal of

Roe v. Wade and laws banning contraception or homosexuality, may be challenged and overturned as a result of appeals to international tribunals.

CONCERNS ABOUT the political influence of the religious right have been raised recently at the European Parliament. The influence of the Christian Coalition in the U.S. and the Vatican at the UN was the motive behind a seminar organized in Brussels in November 2001 by members of the European Parliament.[66] The imminent acceptance of Catholic countries, namely, Poland, the Czech Republic, and Slovakia, as members of the EU has caused concern that they will work in concert with the Vatican to exert pressure on the European Union to roll back provisions on equality for women and for gays and lesbians and on reproductive rights. The Vatican has already leveled harsh criticism at the Charter of Fundamental Human Rights adopted by the European Union in December 2000. Cardinal Camillo Ruini, a close associate of John Paul II, stated that "it failed to take account of the historical and cultural roots of Europe, in particular Christianity, which represents Europe's soul and which still today can inspire Europe's mission and identity." The particular focus of his concern were the provisions of the charter granting equal rights to homosexuals.

In March 2002, despite a campaign of opposition orchestrated by the Vatican, the European Parliament passed a resolution condemning religious fundamentalism. It reaffirmed the separation of church and state as central to the ideals of democracy and established that women's equality in every aspect of life is a positive value of modern society. It also criticized the Vatican for denying women a place within the hierarchy of the church and for attempting to assert control over women's sexuality. Religious freedom must remain subject to universal rights; religions cannot claim exemption from the UN Charter of Rights. The EU will now be in a position to provide a voice of reason to counteract the influence of Christian and Islamic fundamentalists at the UN.

Conservative Catholic strategy at the UN involves the use of the Holy See's status as a state to block progress toward women's equality and introduce language into UN documents which would advance the demands of pro-family groups.[67] The Cairo Conference on Population and Development (1994) not only saw the birth of the UN pro-family movement, Ruse has written, "it also saw the emergence of a new and very potent alliance between Catholic and Muslim countries. Our enemies see all this as an unholy alliance. And so from their point of view it is, because it is from this alliance, new to the world, new to history, that our victory will come."[68]

The leadership of the pro-family coalition at the UN emerged from groups already seasoned by their work inserting the Moral Majority into U.S. domestic politics. Conservative Protestant Evangelicals from the Howard Institute on the Family, Religion and Society established in Rockford, Illinois, in 1997 have joined with the Family Research Center, Conservative Catholics from the C-FAM outgrowth from HLI, and Mormons from the World Family Policy Center at Brigham Young University.[69] These groups sponsored two meetings of the World Congress of Families, one in Prague in 1997 and the other in Geneva in the fall of 1999, with the aim of responding to "the organized efforts at the United Nations and other international agencies to discredit or deny traditional family life. The statement of purpose adopted by the group states that "the natural family is established by the Creator and essential to a good society, . . . the fundamental social unit inscribed in human nature and centered on the voluntary union of man and woman in the lifelong covenant of marriage . . . and procreation."[70]

Their "natural family" excludes homosexuals, even though these latter are the products of so-called "natural" families. The Howard Institute, along with other elements of the Catholic and Evangelical right, blames homosexuals and Jews, as well as feminists, for the woes of modern society. "Two European Jews" stated the Howard Institute's May 2000 Religion and Society Report, "Karl Marx and Sigmund Freud, played a major role in the secularization of culture, launching major assaults on the God of the Bible and leading countless Jews and Gentiles into skepticism and unbelief." Pat Robertson and Jerry Falwell held feminists and lesbians responsible for provoking God to organize the Muslim fundamentalists to bomb the World Trade Center on September 11, 2001, because they are responsible for the decline in morality in America. The Howard Institute holds Jews themselves responsible for the Nazi Holocaust, which, they say, was a "clear sign of God's wrath at broken covenants."[71] It is frightening to imagine that groups with this warped view of history should consider themselves arbiters of the future direction of the world by intervening at the UN.

Working in concert with the Holy See, they aim especially to influence delegates from the developing world. That the Vatican should pose as the defender of the third world and its indigenous peoples betrays a cynical attitude toward history. The Vatican's historical record includes blessing, and sometimes organizing, colonial campaigns of genocide against indigenous cultures in North and South. And now the Vatican, run by elderly white males, continues to campaign against equal rights for women, contraception, and AIDS prevention in poor countries where the Catholic Church still has influence, knowing full well that these battles have been lost in the developed world. It is white Protestant Christian groups from the dominant economic classes of the United States, whose government's economic policies have reduced many third world countries to the verge of bankruptcy, who are now allies of the Vatican in this cynical attempt to manipulate public opinion by presenting themselves as the new face of compassion and advocacy for the poor.

Not only does the Vatican fail to disassociate itself from extremist groups; it actively encourages them. John Paul II has praised Human Life International for doing "the most important work on earth."[72] The Catholic Church flirts with strange bedfellows whose literature recounts lurid scenarios of plots against America equated to plots against God, apocalyptic prophecies, and the violent Christianity of Randall Terry: "We're losing the fight, friends. I am a general in this war and I would be ill-serving if I did not tell you the truth. We're not just losing. We're getting our tails whipped, and it's not just happening in America.... Why are we losing?... We are losing because of a lack of strong, righteous, courageous, visionary Christian leadership. The USA and the nations represented here tonight...we're locked into a cultural civil war."[73] One of the major theaters of this "cultural civil war" of right-wing church groups and the international community is the struggle of women to realize full equality with men in all spheres of life, not excluding the churches. It is thus not surprising that many leaders of conservative groups such as Opus Dei, HLI, Operation Rescue, the Moral Majority, and, of course, the Catholic Church itself, are men. Much of the Vatican's opposition to feminism and to the extension of women's rights at the international level reflects its attempt to douse the fire of the fierce struggle taking place within the Catholic Church over the admission of women to priesthood. Rome's argument against women priests is not firmly rooted in scripture and rests on the acceptance of intrinsic differences between male and female human nature and the inability of a female human being to represent Jesus Christ. Hence the vociferous opposition of the Holy See to the use of the concept of gender as a tool of analysis and the insistence that women's nature as determined by God demands that they fulfill their destiny primarily through biological motherhood.

Right-wing Christian groups refuse to accept that gender is a cultural and social as well as a biological construct. "Underlying their concerns [about the traditional family] is an outrage at the feminist assertion that gender is a social construct that benefits men at the expense of women. According to one pro-family advocate, 'The abolition of this sexual division of labor amounts to the abolition of motherhood.' "[74] And so the "private" life of the family has become the arena of struggle for right-wing groups in both Catholic and Protestant churches. Christian morality focused on the private lives of individuals (their acceptance of Jesus Christ in the case of Protestants or their adherence to orthodox beliefs about abortion and birth control in the case of Catholics) has fostered a self-absorption which turns a blind eye toward the systemic injustices inherent in the Western economic system. Christianity and the profit-driven economy are fueling the same self-absorbed ideology. The call for a return to the values of the patriarchal family omits the issue of the economic dependence of the middle-class nuclear family in the United States, Canada, and Europe on the sweatshop labor and the discriminatory, sometimes death-dealing, labor practices of American multinationals in the third world. The privatized Christianity of the right, which prides itself on the preservation of family values at home, exists in a comfortable bubble of self-satisfaction, divorced from the life of the two-thirds of the human family who are poor.

This is one reason that this privatized, consumer-friendly Christianity has such mass appeal. Once a person has undergone a personal "conversion" and "accepted the Lord Jesus" into his or her life, then the problems of society are projected onto "the others," the feminists, gays and lesbians, or communists. What Girard described as the mimetic desire for conformity, with its need to focus outside itself on a common enemy or victim regarded as a threat to the preservation of the system, is apparent in Catholic and Protestant fundamentalist groups.

THE APPEAL of mass conformity is also powerfully at work in the gatherings known as Catholic World Youth Days. The first Youth Day was held in Rome in 1984. Since then, a total of sixteen have been held in different cities including Buenos Aires, Manila, Paris, and Denver. The appeal of World Youth Days, especially to the Catholic hierarchy, is the sense of mass compliance they generate and the opportunity of access to a large captive audience.

On one level, the Youth Days represent a Disneyfication of the Catholic Church. The elaborate mass meetings, the medieval costumes of pope and cardinals and bishops, the limos, the elaborate receptions by state and municipal politicians, all this makes for good media and Hollywood spectacle. At its climax, the pope descends from the sky to bless the crowd. To the superficial observer, it could seem like a relatively harmless tourist attraction. But underneath the pageantry, there is a tightly controlled agenda that is designed to prevent the raising of critical questions or the admission of voices of diversity and pluralism within the church. Events are carefully orchestrated to prevent any semblance of dissent or even democracy. Youth are to be "catechized" during the days. Catechetics, as opposed to education, is from the same root as "catechism." It involves giving the answers — and only one set of preauthorized "right" answers — to preselected questions. It is a top-down teaching technique which, at the Youth Days, will be performed only by bishops.

And when the bishops have packed up their robes and returned to their palaces, life will go back to normal. The church will not have provided young people with real answers because it has refused to listen to their real questions. This may explain why surveys suggest that the majority of young people still believe in God, but fewer than 20 percent of them attend church.[75] Over 66 percent of Canadians aged eighteen to thirty-five, the same age range as those invited to attend the Papal Youth Days, identify themselves as Christian. But their faith, in the words of one sociologist of religion, has become "unlocked from the church."[76]

Ten years ago, a comprehensive study of youth in Catholic high schools in Toronto was carried out under the aegis of the Institute for Catholic Education, or ICE, as it is known. The report was commissioned ten years after the government of the province of Ontario passed legislation extending the public funding of Catholic schools to the end of high school. This meant that religion could be taught at every level of the high school curriculum.

The objectives of the survey were twofold. The first was to "take stock of the extent to which agreement [on the objectives of the Catholic school system] exists among the various groups that make up the Anglophone Catholic community. The second was to "determine the extent to which Grade 12 students in Ontario Anglophone Catholic separate schools conform to these objectives."[77] The survey included bishops, priests, school trustees, teachers, parents, and a sampling of Grade 12 students. The students were given a battery of questions to test their knowledge of the Catholic faith and how this affected their attitudes and behavior. In terms of knowledge, students showed a high level of correct answers (i.e., in conformity to the teachings of the church) to ethical questions about marriage, the church's teachings on sexuality and birth control and ethical action in general.[78] "One could expect," the report continues, "a relationship to exist between religious knowledge and the importance of religion to the individual. Such is not the case."[79] Neither is it the case that student membership in Catholic organizations, such as third world justice, parish, or pro-life groups correlates with the level of student involvement in the church. If students belong to any organization (and the majority do not), most favor environmental organizations. The Blishen report adds: "In view of the Church's teaching about abortion, one could expect that students would favor membership in organizations opposing it, but such is not the case. . . . Students with a higher level of religious knowledge are more likely to be members of organizations with the exception of organizations opposing abortion, in which case the most knowledgeable are more likely *not* to join."

The conclusions of the Blishen Report are echoed in a recent study that investigated the impact of today's social, economic, and cultural changes on the religious and moral consciousness of young people aged eighteen to thirty in six Western countries: Britain, the United States, Italy, Malta, Poland, and Ireland.[80] The study found that while there is still a core of committed young Catholics in each country, their religious orientation differs. In the pluralist countries of Britain and the United States, the young adults have come to exercise their faith in a questioning, semi-autonomous fashion. Those who remain committed to the church are, by and large, progressive and support internal reform in the church. In the other four formerly Catholic countries, family pressures and traditional viewpoints exercise a stronger hold over youth, who are thus less likely to challenge the church.

In contrast to the right-wing prescription of a more authoritarian and absolutist approach as a cure for what they view as the malaise of youth raised in postmodern democratic and inclusive societies,

Fulton argues that the more pluralist the society, the more mature is the faith of young believers. Questioning the church does not imply a lack of faith: it is, he argues, an essential step toward adult belief. It is the authoritarian approach of the right-wing movements and of Youth Days which leads to a less firmly rooted faith because it is induced from without and produces only a temporary and superficial conformity.

These radically differing assessments of the influence of the modern world on youth reflect the deeper issues of the debate within all the Christian churches today about the role of religion in the postmodern world. Authoritarian Christian denominations like Catholicism and evangelical Protestantism have responded to the challenge by falling back on fostering mimetic conformity among their followers. The Ratzinger and Robertson versions of Christianity paint the modern world as a hostile backdrop for the church. The world places the churches on the defensive lest they be beguiled by its perversion of the truth. The pluralistic modern democratic state is regarded as inimical because it treats groups such as women, gays and lesbians, and non-Christians as equal partakers in the kingdom. The focus of the conversion preached by the churches is on its external enemies. The need for the church itself to be converted is brushed aside, as is any internal dissent.

But another mounting pressure from within for the Catholic Church is to place its own victims at the center of its consciousness. The Catholic hierarchy has closed the doors on the internal transformation of the church envisioned by Vatican II. Now the voices of the church's own victims are crying out for it to recognize its internal dysfunction. Despite the pope's apologies for some of the wrongs committed in the past, its checkered history has not taught the Vatican humility. If the "unchanging" truths taught by the church in the past have led to pogroms, crusades, extermination of native peoples, and burning of witches, then surely the church should be somewhat hesitant in still asserting that it alone possesses absolute and unchanging truth. It would behoove Catholics to exercise more humility in the face of history.

The continuing revelations of pedophilia among Catholic priests all over the world and the recent unearthing of the terrible history of the abuse of native children in church-run residential schools in Canada are a stark reminder of what can happen when Christianity chooses to proclaim itself as the only route to God and demands an unfettered access to youth on the part of its ministers. The initial denial of the sexual abuse of children and the stubborn resistance to accept culpability on the part of the adults concerned is the terrible outcome of a system caught up in the mimetic contagion of violence. It is this same frightening ethos behind the sectarian movements in the church today which cultivate secrecy, stealth tactics, lying, and covert approaches to minors, and brook neither questioning nor accountability in regard to their actions.

The past twenty years of external Catholic triumphalism have witnessed its internal unraveling, as the widespread history of sexual abuse by Catholic priests has been unfolding all over the world. The heinous treatment by the church of its own abused youth belies its professed concern for the welfare of youth in general. While Catholic leaders have been condemning the sexual depravity of the rest of the world, they have ignored, denied, and downplayed the disgraceful conduct of their own clergy. The voices of the victims of abuse within the church call for its conversion away from a violent, arrogant, and judgmental proclamation of the truth toward a more compassionate and humble orientation to God and the world.

FIVE

Pedophilia and Sexual Abuse: The Terrible Legacy of the Church's Abuse of Power

It was late spring 1991. I had just returned from Holland, where I had been attending a meeting of church reform groups, the Acht mei Beweging, or Eighth of May Movement. I had been invited to talk about the meeting to a group of people gathered at the home of friends in the Catholic reform movement who live near Mar, Ontario. This was close to the boundary of the native reserve of Nayaushingnming, also known by its English name as Cape Croker. As the evening drew to a close over coffee and dessert, three women approached me. They were native women from the reserve. One of them, Stella, was an elder. They asked me if I would come to Nayaushingnming the next morning to meet with some people from the community.

The next morning I set off for Stella's house. On the way I passed by magnificent tree-covered cliffs which descended into the pure blue waters of Lake Huron. Her house was on the main street of the reserve, just past the church. There were six people waiting inside, two men and four women. We sat down with cups of coffee and one of the men began to speak. "We wanted you to come and hear Dan's story," he said, indicating the younger man with a nod of his head. "We're trying to get something done about Dan's situation, and because you're involved in the church reform movement we thought you could help us decide what to do next."

"The community is very divided about it," added Stella, "and we were wondering if you knew what other people in similar circumstances have been able to do in situations like ours." Dan is an Ojibway man with fine features and gentle brown eyes who was then in his late twenties. "I was born here on the reserve," he began. "I

123

was baptized because my parents were Catholics, and when I was ten I became an altar boy. I loved it because there was a whole group of us boys who would hang around the church together. My parents were both alcoholics so there wasn't much for me at home. The priest used to give us cigarettes and treats, and he had a TV so we used to go there in the evening to watch it.

"One by one," he continued, "Father began inviting us to stay over. When it was my turn to go, I was excited about it because his place was so much cleaner and nicer than my home and the others told me he always made a good breakfast in the morning." Dan sighed and started to speak very softly. I dreaded what I was going to hear next. "First Father asked me to take a bath," he continued. "He got the soap and washed me himself. Then he gave me clean pajamas and tucked me up in bed. A little while later I heard him come into the room and then he got into bed with me. "Don't worry, Dan," he said. "I only want to hold you close."

Then he turned me on my side with my back to him. He put one arm around me and started stroking me. Then he got hold of my penis and started fondling it. "This is my cock," he'd say. "These are my balls." I could hear him grunting and then he let out a large groan. Then he told me to go to sleep, and he left me alone. But the next morning he came back and did the same thing."

Dan's sister Mary broke in: "This priest chose only the boys who had problems at home. He knew they wouldn't say anything to their parents, and even if they did, the parents wouldn't do anything about it. He only picked on certain boys who were the most vulnerable." "I guess we all knew it was happening to each of us," added Stan. "We'd talk about it in school the next day. Father would always give us treats and make a big fuss over us." This priest abused a total of fifteen boys. Their ages at the time ranged from eight to fourteen.

Dan then described how the priest gradually initiated him into sex and how this took place regularly all through his early adolescence. He shifted in his chair. "You know what the worst thing is about this?" he said. "It's not so much dealing with the shame of what happened to me. I've been very lucky to find a wife who is helping me to come to terms with the fact that I'm not guilty for what Father did, and it wasn't my fault for leading him on or anything. It's the way it's affected my relationship with my baby boy. I just can't bathe him or hold him naked without all these horrible memories coming back and feeling that I'm some kind of pervert."

By this time everyone had tears in their eyes. I could not speak—
I had no words with which to respond to the terrible pathos of his
story. After a few minutes Stella spoke up. "The community is divided
about what to do about Dan and the other boys who were abused.
That priest is dead now, and some of the older people don't want any
public airing of these stories. They're afraid it will bring shame on
our community, and they say we should move on and let it rest. But
some of us think that for the sake of the victims, there should be a
public hearing and an apology from the church."

The eventual outcome of the situation was that after much soul-
searching and discussion, the community did decide to confront the
superiors of the religious order to which this priest belonged with
the truth about what he had done. A year later, after a long and
painful process, the order apologized and the victims received some
compensation. I had several subsequent phone conversations with
Stella and Dan, and they kept me updated about the course of their
struggle to speak the truth to power.

That chance but fortuitous encounter with Stella would take me
down another unmarked road on my life's journey. Like others who
were led into a far country, I found my destination to be not the
court of a king but the company of the poor. The star led the Magi
away from the center of power and influence in Herod's court to a
place where no one would have imagined that a God could be born.
Then the star led them back to their own country by an unknown,
different way. Soon afterward, this divine birth in a stable become
a sign of contradiction and opposition for the religious and secular
powers of the time. Stella's invitation, like others that I have received
from those who have suffered abuse at the hands of the Catholic
Church, have continued to lead me back to engage the church by
circuitous, controversial, and sometimes confrontational routes. It
has not turned out to be the journey of faith that I had originally
envisaged myself taking.

Some of my closest friends are Catholic priests, and I hold them in
high regard and deep affection. Speaking out about sexual abuse in
the church is not something I would ever have wished upon myself,
but nevertheless I now accept that it has become part of my call to
discipleship. My new route to engaging the church on this issue has
led me into the heart of a struggle that is taking place deep within
Catholicism. It is one where issues of integrity versus influence, of
truth versus power, are bitterly contested.

This moving encounter in Nayaushingnming, Ontario, was not the first time I had met with Catholic survivors of clerical sexual abuse. Two years before this, the revelations of sexual abuse at Mount Cashel in Newfoundland had started to appear in the Canadian media. As a result of the testimonies of former residents of the orphanage and others who had been abused in parishes in the Archdiocese of St. John's, a whole network of collusion, secrecy, and denial of the abuse among church leaders, social services, and police was exposed. All the agencies charged with their protection had, at one time or another, conspired against the young victims in order to uphold the power of the church.

Church leaders have failed to recognize the face of the suffering Christ revealed in the victims of sexual abuse. Of all the issues confronting the Catholic Church, that of sexual abuse by its clergy is crucial to the conflict between integrity and influence within the church. When the history of the Catholic Church of this time comes to be written by future generations, the scandalous way that the institution has responded to its own victims will be seen as the most potent catalyst for reform within the church. Of all the recent abuses of power in the church — whether through the sanctioning of ultra-conservative groups, the silencing of theological diversity, or the continuing oppression of women — the cover-up and denial of criminal sexual acts on the part of priests against children has to be the most heinous.

There are three scenarios of the abuse of power by the church that have come to light within Catholic communities all over the world over the past thirty years. One is the abuse of vulnerable youth in parishes and church-run institutions. Another is the abuse of native children in church-run residential schools. Then there are the recent revelations of the sexual abuse of nuns by Catholic priests, mainly in the developing world.

It must be acknowledged that incidents of the sexual abuse of minors are by no means confined to the Catholic Church, nor are Catholic priest offenders the only category of persons who have been placed in a position of authority and then abused their trust in this manner. Clergy in other faiths and Christian denominations, doctors, teachers, coaches: individuals within all of these categories have all been found guilty of unspeakable acts of abuse perpetrated against children. But within the Catholic Church, the effect of the actual acts of abuse have been magnified for the victims by the extent to which the brotherhood of priests and bishops has closed ranks in denial, cover-up, and protection for the offenders.

SEXUAL ABUSE is as much about power as it is about sex. Catholic priest-abusers share many of the characteristics of others who select their victims from among the ranks of children and adolescents. But the priest-offender lives in a context where an almost unlimited access to young people is also harnessed to the restraint on adult sexual relationships imposed by the vow of celibacy that is a condition for ordination. For some priests, this volatile mix has provided a situation conducive to abuse. In some parts of the world where Catholicism is the religion of the majority of people, the social services and the justice system have exhibited an unseemly degree of deference toward priests, which has provided a context where secrecy about clerical sins can flourish. In Newfoundland, what would turn out to be one of the most shocking situations of serial sexual abuse at Mount Cashel was initially investigated in 1975, but the investigation lasted only one week and was dropped on the order of the then deputy police chief.[1]

One of the first cases of sexual abuse by a Catholic priest to receive widespread public attention was that of Fr. Gilbert Gauthe in Louisiana. Starting in the 1970s, Gauthe molested almost one hundred boys in four different parishes in the southern United States. In 1984, after a group of parents pressed civil charges, the police investigated and Gauthe was charged. In 1985 he was sentenced to twenty years imprisonment. A Catholic judge awarded him early parole for good conduct in 1998. Later the same year, Gauthe was arrested once again for molesting a teenage boy and placed on probation. This early case opened the window of scrutiny on sexual abuse, and by the end of 1985, forty priests in the U.S. had been charged with sexual offenses against minors. By 1987, there were 135 allegations. In 1985, a confidential report drawn up for the U.S. Conference of Catholic Bishops drew attention to the serious implications of failing to report abuse to the secular authorities. One of its authors, Fr. Thomas Doyle, addressing the Canon Law Society of America in 1986, spoke of this as "the most serious crisis that we in the church have faced for centuries."[2] His words have proved tragically prophetic. In the United States, prosecutions of abuse by clergy now number thousands of cases and the church's liability for compensation to the victims runs into millions of dollars. The Archdiocese of Los Angeles and the Diocese of Orange in California, for example, recently settled a $5.2 million lawsuit brought by a young man who was abused in high school by his priest-principal, Fr. Michael Harris, in 1991.

In 1985, a report on the extent of pedophilia among U.S. priests known as "The Manual" was presented to the U.S. Conference of Catholic Bishops. Fr. Michael Peterson, a priest-psychiatrist, Fr. Thomas Doyle, a canon lawyer, and Ray Mouton, a former attorney who had defended Gauthe, authored it. Their report recommends that the church take the initiative to reach out to the victims; otherwise it would face a deluge of lawsuits. The emphasis, as always, was on avoiding scandal for the church, not on the welfare of the victims. The report also recommended the establishment of a national policy group to create mandatory, uniform procedures on clergy sex abuse in all U.S. dioceses. The bishops were briefed on the report, but they never followed through on its recommendations. Doyle commented later: "The report was rejected. Somebody at the NCCB must have decided that it was too threatening or too controversial and it was dropped."[3] It was not until 1993 that the U.S. National Conference of Catholic Bishops, facing exactly the pressure from lawsuits that the authors of the report had foreseen, established a committee on sexual abuse.

The work of this committee does not appear to have had much impact on changing the scandalous lack of concern for children manifested by the church's pastors. As recently as January 2002, former priest John J. Geoghan faced the first of two criminal trials for raping and sexually abusing children. Geoghan the priest chose his victims carefully, often from families where a single mother was struggling to care for a number of children and welcomed his apparent pastoral support. One of his alleged victims was four years old at the time of the assault. A total of eighty-four civil lawsuits against Geoghan are pending. Cardinal Bernard Law, archbishop of Boston, knew about Geoghan's predatory sexual inclinations since 1984 but simply moved him around from parish to parish throughout the 1980s and 1990s every time concerns about his activities surfaced.[4] Six other priests in the Archdiocese of Boston had been suspended on accusations of sexually abusing children only two weeks after Cardinal Law had denied that there were any other active priests in the diocese facing charges.[5]

Law's reprehensible conduct and the implication in the cover-ups of other prominent U.S. churchmen, such as Cardinal Egan of New

York, has caused the simmering scandal of sexual abuse in the church to boil over again. Bishop O'Connell of Palm Beach recently resigned after admitting to sexual abuse of a student. A Polish bishop, Julius Paetz of Poznan, is under pressure to resign after reports about his sexual misconduct surfaced in the Polish media. The hundreds of new cases of abuse that are surfacing will provide the impetus for reform in a priesthood that is now discredited and demoralized.

In 1988, reports surfaced in the Canadian media about the sexual and physical abuse of boys at the orphanage of Mount Cashel in St. John's, Newfoundland, run by the Christian Brothers. Allegations of sexual misconduct against priests in the same city and elsewhere in Newfoundland also surfaced. As a result of public outcry, Archbishop Alphonsus L. Penney of St. John's set up a commission of enquiry to examine why it had happened and to come up with recommendations for preventing its occurrence in the future. The two volumes of its report, known as the Winter Commission Report after its chair, former lieutenant governor of Newfoundland Gordon Winter, were published in June 1990.[6]

The commissioners traveled throughout this very Catholic Canadian province and heard depositions from individuals and groups throughout Newfoundland. These included priests, religious sisters, lay people, and entire parish councils. It also incorporated studies from professionals in the area of sexual abuse, which analyzed the various factors — individual, familial, societal, cultural, and religious — which contribute to the profile of an individual abuser. "Allegations of child sexual abuse," the report states, "were reported to officials of the Archdiocese in 1975.... Despite this awareness, Archdiocesan authorities seem to have followed a minimum response policy."[7] While it acknowledges that public awareness and knowledge of the dynamics of sexual abuse were more limited in the 1970s than today, the Winter Commission's analysis of the factors that contributed to its occurrence drew attention to the "particular factors related to the Church which had a bearing on the occurrence of sexual abuse."[8]

"Child sexual abuse," it continues,

> is a deviant act based on power and manipulation. When priests of the Archdiocese sexually abused children, they exploited special power that derived from their positions as spiritual and community leaders.... This pattern of power left the priest in the parish with too much influence, unchecked by the social —

and sometimes legal — balances. It precluded a healthy skepticism about the men who occupied positions of authority in the Church.... The public perception about the position of the clergy also led to the isolation of the priest and his inability to integrate socially with parishioners.... Much of this misuse of power and the misunderstanding of the right relationship between priests and parishioners is the result of the poor ecclesiology within the Archdiocese. Neither the priests nor the lay members of the Archdiocese have been adequately led to the vision of the Church which continues to emanate from the Second Vatican Council.[9]

The vision of the church emanating from the Second Vatican Council has now become a major area of conflict within the Catholic Church. The Winter Commission in 1990 put its collective finger on a sensitive fault line in the church. Thus it provides a vital link between an analysis of sexual abuse by priests and other examples flowing from the dysfunctional exercise of power in the church that I have analyzed in previous chapters.

The report summarized the issues which must be addressed under five headings: power; education; sexuality and the priesthood; the structures of the parish; and management within the archdiocese. Power in the Catholic Church, it states, "is seen as the prerogative of the clergy."[10] "Closely associated with this kind of power is the concept of patriarchy.... Many have argued that patriarchal thinking is one of the contributing factors to the sexual abuse of children because of the power and position it confers upon the members of the patriarchal establishment, in particular the ordained clergy."[11] The report states that the "patriarchal establishment" in the church is paternalistic and sexist. In his recent book, *The Changing Face of the Catholic Priesthood*, Donald Cozzens, rector and professor of pastoral theology at St. Mary's Seminary in Cleveland, Ohio, points out that it has traditionally been mothers who have fostered vocations to the priesthood in the Catholic Church. This is no longer the case. "The paternalistic attitudes," Cozzens concludes, quoting another source, "the increasing consciousness of women, the lack of appreciation for the value of celibacy, the large percentage of gay priests, the pedophilia crisis, all have so impacted our recruitment efforts that I see no possibility of salvaging the priesthood as we know it today."[12]

According to the Winter Commission, the power of church leaders to stifle dissent contributed to their denial of wrongdoing and the silencing of the victims which characterized the church's initial response to sexual abuse. Steadfast refusal to acknowledge the misdeeds of the clergy is part and parcel of the same mindset that has fostered the rise of authoritarian right-wing movements within the church. The silencing of discussion on theological issues and a resort to authority to enforce consent results in a culture of subservience to the hierarchy on the part of lay people. This all too characteristically Catholic docility, the Winter Commission Report points out, is inculcated early in the lives of young Catholics with their experience of attending a denominational school. The church's administrative role in Catholic schools leads to a suppression of discussion on controversial issues in the classroom such as male dominance, violence against women and children, women's ordination, and sexuality and gender roles. This leaves Catholic children and youth especially vulnerable to abuse and also inhibits them from coming forward to report it.[13]

Compulsory celibacy is cited as a factor that has contributed to immature sexual development, which can lead to furtive and dysfunctional sexual relationships on the part of priests who cannot live up to this requirement. The rule of celibacy dates only from the twelfth century as a requirement for Catholic clergy and was abandoned in Protestant churches as a result of the Reformation four hundred years later. The Winter Commission acknowledges that celibacy, in and of itself, does not lead to sexual abuse. Nevertheless, it states, "the commission has deep concern, in the face of the evidence it has assembled, that there has been a long and disturbing anxiety within the presbyterium (group of priests) relating to the observance of priestly celibacy."[14] Recommendation #54 of the Commission offers this solution: "that the Archbishop [of St. John's] join with other bishops across Canada to address fully, directly, honestly and without reservation questions relating to the problematic link between celibacy and the ministerial priesthood."[15]

More than a decade has passed since that recommendation was issued and the discussion has yet to take place, either in Canada or anywhere in the universal church. Sexual abuse is not confined to the past: it is still happening in Catholic institutions. So is the denial of its effects. Catholic bishops are still reassigning convicted child abusers to parishes where they are in contact with youth. In February 2002, Rev. James Kneale, convicted of sexually assaulting a sixteen-year-old boy in Niagara Falls, Ontario, in 1999, and having served a conditional sentence, was reassigned to St. Patrick's Parish in Calgary. The vicar general for the Calgary diocese stated that Bishop Fred Henry of Calgary was aware of Kneale's past when he hired him and placed him in another parish. According to Bishop Henry, Kneale had paid for his crime and deserved to be forgiven.[16] The victims were not asked for their opinion on this, nor were Kneale's parishioners consulted as to whether they would be willing to place their children at risk in order to assist with their pastor's rehabilitation.

Author Donald Cozzens also laments the fact that the leadership of the church is not yet open and mature enough to have a full and open discussion on the systemic issues related to abuse and mandatory celibacy. "To insist that there is simply no correlation between mandatory celibacy and the present crisis of clergy misconduct with minors looks like bureaucratic bullying as long as the Vatican remains opposed to even discussion concerning the systems undergirding the priestly lifestyle."[17] This bureaucratic bullying is yet another indication of what happens when the power of truth falls victim to the "truths" promulgated by power.

Bullying was often the first tactic the church in Newfoundland used in order to try to silence the voices of the victims. "The Church . . . showed little compassion toward the victims. Church officials aligned themselves with the accused: their response to the victims was inappropriate and un-Christian, and this compounded the victims' initial sense of betrayal by the Church."[18] The actual abuse by individual clergy was further compounded by others placed in positions of pastoral care by the church. Children and adolescents, already betrayed by priests in a position of trust, found themselves doubly victimized at the hands of the system that closed ranks in order to shelter the perpetrators. To the victims, it seemed as though the whole church colluded in fabricating truth under the delusion that by lies and denial the leaders would ensure the preservation of its power.

An example of collusion with abuse that reaches to the highest level of the church was recently exposed in the *National Catholic Reporter.*[19] This case involves accusations of abuse against Fr. Marcial Maciel Degollado, the founder of the conservative order of priests known as the Legionaries of Christ. Nine former members of the Legion, including a retired priest in good standing and three university professors, began to petition the Vatican for a hearing in 1978. Another letter was sent to the pope in 1989, but with no response.

Maciel is a personal friend of John Paul II, recently praised by the pope as "an efficacious guide to youth."[20] To John Paul II, the Legion is a shining example of his new orthodoxy, a herald of the new evangelization of youth, and a defense against the moral relativism of the world. This was after Maciel was accused of initiating sexual relationships with his former seminarians, some as young as ten years old. The victims have tried to bring a case against him under the church's Code of Canon Law. They accuse Maciel of transgressing Canon 1378 by violating the sacrament of confession by granting absolution to victims of his own sexual misconduct. If proven guilty, he would be excommunicated.

In 1997, stories of the accusations against Maciel were carried in the U.S. and Mexican media. A year later Archbishop Justo Mullor, the papal nuncio in Mexico, assured the victims that their letters had been given to John Paul II. They engaged the services of a canon lawyer in Rome, and early in 1999, the Congregation for the Doctrine of the Faith gave permission for the case to proceed. Then in December 1999, the defendants were abruptly informed that the Vatican had quashed the case against Maciel. At the time, the church court had examined none of the evidence, nor had it heard the victims' depositions. The defendants were advised to file a civil suit against Maciel.

In January 2000, on the occasion of the sixtieth anniversary of the Legion, Pope John Paul II publicly honored Maciel before a cheering crowd of supporters in St. Peter's Square. He greeted him "with special affection" stating that "he especially appreciated his confirmation of your characteristic fidelity to the successor of St. Peter."[21] The Maciel case is a stark indication of the corruption of absolute power that has compromised the integrity of the highest levels of the Catholic Church. The victims, having struggled for years to follow due process within the church, were cynically told that they would have been better off all along seeking justice from secular courts. Shortly after this incident, the Vatican feted Maciel for his fidelity to the pope. This was during the Year of Jubilee 2000, when the pope apologized publicly and profusely for the past sins of the church.

IN 1989, Margaret Kennedy, a disability and child protection consultant in London, England, founded CSSA, Christian Survivors of Sexual Abuse. In a recent article in the *Child Abuse Review,* she writes, "It is a myth that Christian communities...are safer than

secular communities! To be 'holy' or to be connected to holiness was
to be perceived as safe."[22] Quoting Bishop Jamison of New Zealand,
Kennedy continues: "All the other bishops . . . all male, who have been
called upon to deal with incidents of clergy misconduct have found
it incredibly hard to break the bonds of brotherhood with their male
colleagues and ensure a just outcome by taking steps to terminate the
priests' license for ministry." It is a sad commentary on how far the
church has strayed from the truth, to acknowledge that it has only
been prosecution by the secular courts that has been able to shake
these bonds of brotherhood.

Time and again, victims who have had recourse to what should be
the pastoral care of their bishop have been denied a proper hearing,
bought off and sometimes even roundly rebuked for their temerity.
In 1994, Eugene LaRocque, the bishop of Alexandria-Cornwall, Ontario, admitted that the church had paid $32,000 in 1992 to bribe
a victim to withdraw charges of sexual abuse against a priest. Despite a protest from Cornwall's chief of police to the papal nuncio,
the priest remained in his assignment until news of the bribe broke in
1994. When first confronted by the media with the story of the bribe,
LaRocque lied and denied the payment had been made, but later he
changed his story and admitted the truth.[23]

The secular courts also recently removed another excuse for the
evasion of episcopal responsibility toward children. In the town of
Caen in northern France, a priest, Fr. René Bissey, was sentenced
to eighteen years in jail in February 2001 for the repeated rape of
one boy and the sexual abuse of ten others over a period of seven
years, between 1989 and 1996. A further list of offenses by Fr. Bissey
dating back to the 1970s was not brought to trial because the time
lapse had exceeded the statute of limitations. It emerged that several
years before his arrest, the priest had made a sacramental confession
of these crimes to his bishop. But instead of reporting him to the
authorities, the bishop simply sent him on retreat for six months,
and then assigned him to another parish. This has been a depressingly
familiar pattern of how church authorities have tried to hide the truth
about clerical sexual abuse. Thanks to the intervention of secular
courts, this may soon come to an end.

When the court threatened to place Bishop Pierre Pican, Bissey's
superior, on trial for covering up offenses against minors, he at first
pleaded innocence on account of the inviolable secrecy of the confessional. He argued that he felt that the grace of the sacrament of

confession should have allowed the pedophile priest to "come to the truth about himself and to take the appropriate action."[24] In September 2001, rejecting this claim in favor of its mandate to protect the interests of children, the court sentenced Bishop Pican to a three-month suspended jail sentence. This decision places Catholic bishops everywhere on notice that they will be held liable for failing to deal with sexual abuse even when it is only reported privately within the secrecy of the confessional.

In 1990, guidelines issued by the Canadian Conference of Catholic Bishops for dealing with the reporting of sexual abuse attempted to anticipate this problem by stating that no bishop should hear the confession of a priest suspected of sexual abuse once he has been formally accused.[25] But this did not address the protection afforded to the priest and bishop in canon law if the priest confessed before being arraigned in a secular court. Now, in the case of the abuse of children, this protection for clergy provided in canon law has been overridden.

The failure of bishops to exercise their ministry of pastoral care toward children has also been highlighted by the revelations of sexual abuse by Catholic clergy in England and Wales. Over the past five years, nearly one hundred priests have been investigated for crimes of sexual abuse against children, and close to thirty have been convicted. In a case that resonates tragically with similar situations in Canada and the United States, the then Archbishop of Arundel and Brighton, Cormac Murphy-O'Connor, moved a priest, Fr. Michael Hill, whom he knew was an abuser, from parish to parish for nineteen years. After complaints about Hill's conduct with boys in the parish of Heathfield, Murphy-O'Connor sent the priest away for therapy and then reassigned him to be chaplain at Gatwick Airport. There Hill assaulted a child with learning disabilities and was finally charged. He was convicted and spent five years in jail.

Archbishop John Ward of Cardiff recently ordained a former teacher who he knew had already been convicted of six charges of sexual assault and barred from teaching. The archbishop withheld this key information about the candidate from members of the diocesan selection board. The candidate, Joe Jordan, had been training for the priesthood in the diocese of Plymouth, but Bishop Budd of Plymouth had decided to advise him to withdraw from the seminary. Notwithstanding this directive, Jordan transferred to Cardiff and was ordained there in 1998. During the eighteen months after ordination, he indecently assaulted two boys and amassed a library of five hundred pornographic pictures of children on his computer. He was arrested shortly afterward.[26] That same year Archbishop Ward's press spokesperson and close advisor, Fr. John Lloyd, was found guilty of eleven charges of indecent assault, one of rape and one of buggery. Lloyd was already serving a twenty-one-month sentence for sexually assaulting a thirteen-year-old girl just after he had baptized her.

In September 2001, eleven years after the release of the Winter Commission Report in Canada, the Nolan Report was published in England. Its mandate was "to examine and review arrangements made for child protection and the prevention of abuse within the Catholic Church in England and Wales and to make recommendations." Launching the report, Lord Nolan, who chaired the review, described child abuse as "a great evil" and said the church should be "an example of excellence in rooting it out." In a total of eighty-three recommendations, the Nolan Report sets out detailed procedures for the reporting, treatment of the victim and offender, and prevention of abuse.[27]

The report stresses that the church "should be an example of best practice in the prevention of child abuse" and that every parish, diocese, and religious order should have "preventative policies and practices" which will "minimize the opportunity for abuse." The recommendations include a call for every parish to have a designated child protection representative. It also suggests that the Sacrament of Reconciliation for children should be administered so that both priest and child can be visible to but not heard by bystanders. Other key recommendations are that a process for dismissal from the priesthood should automatically be initiated after a priest has been criminally convicted and sentenced to twelve months or more in jail (no. 78); that a child protection coordinator should be appointed for every diocese (no. 10); that the church should impose a unified set of policies on child abuse on both diocesan and monastic clergy, even though canon law does not allow for this (no. 3). The report concludes, "Our hope is that this report will help to bring about a culture of vigilance where every single adult member of the Church consciously and actively takes responsibility for creating a safe environment for children. Our recommendations are not a substitute for this but we hope they will be an impetus toward such an achievement."

In 2001, Cardinal Ratzinger's Congregation for the Doctrine of the Faith suddenly announced that it had assumed jurisdiction over sexual abuse of minors by priests.[28] The new norms require that bishops report suspected cases of child abuse directly to the Congregation. This means that a convicted priest can be more speedily expelled from the priesthood. But because the norms also demand that the cases be tried under the "pontifical secret," the move will result in less accountability to the victims and to the public. There will be more pressure on the victims of sexual abuse to retract the charges, because secrecy will cover both the identity of the accused and the procedure of the court. This new procedure may result in a more efficient method of damage control for the Vatican but in less likelihood of justice for the victims. The preservation of the power of the church and not justice for its victims appears to be the motive for this move.

THE PHENOMENAL NUMBER of cases of priests abusing children has highlighted the abuse of power and truth within the church. Evidence of the abuse of whole groups of children is provided by the history of residential schools in Canada. The first residential schools for aboriginal children were opened in Upper Canada (now the Province of Ontario) in the 1840s. While they were set up and funded by the government of Canada, the administration and teaching in the schools was entrusted to the Christian churches. In 1894, under pressure from the churches, the Canadian government passed an amendment to the Indian Act to make attendance at residential school compulsory for all native children between the ages of seven and fifteen. The Anglican, Presbyterian, United, and Catholic churches were all involved in running the schools, with the Catholic Church having the largest number of schools. More than eighty residential schools were in operation at one time or another in central and western Canada, 67 percent of them operated by the Catholic Church.[29] More than 100,000 native children and youth passed through the residential school system. The last school was closed in 1996.

The goal of the residential schools was to assimilate the aboriginal peoples of Canada into the white culture of their colonizers. "The primary purpose of formal education was to indoctrinate aboriginal people into a Christian, European world view, thereby 'civilizing' them."[30] This was to be achieved by stripping them of their native religion, language, and culture. The "savages," as they were referred to in many documents, were to be transformed into civilized, productive citizens. Once in schools, children often suffered hunger, beatings, and physical abuse as well as sexual abuse at the hands of staff.

Brothers and sisters were separated from each other. Children were forbidden to speak their own languages. They were told that their culture was evil, that they were animals, and that their parents were incapable of taking care of them.

The residential schools also initiated native youth into other aspects of the culture of their colonizers. "We have a lot of pedophiles in our communities," remarked Bob Joseph, chief of the Gwa-wa-enuk band in western Canada "and they learned this in residential school."[31] The cruelty they endured during the day was, for some, intensified by the terror that walked the dormitory by night. The impact of widespread sexual abuse in residential schools magnified their shame over the loss of their land and culture. The long-term results have profoundly marked aboriginal communities. A whole generation of mothers and fathers, cut off from their own parents and their roots, have been bereft of role models for parenting and family life. The cycle of despair has been perpetuated in poverty and alcoholism, as in the story of Dan at the beginning of this chapter. As a result, the legal claims against the churches and the government have been expanded to include the notion of "cultural loss" suffered as a result of the residential school experience.

In 1986, the United Church of Canada became the first Christian church to apologize for the treatment of native children in its schools. "We tried to make you like us," it said, "and in so doing we helped to destroy the vision that made you what you were." It was followed by the Anglican Church in 1993 and a year after this by the Presbyterian Church. Matthew Coon Come, chief of the Assembly of First Nations, has stated that a simple apology does not go far enough.[32] He has suggested that a national Truth and Reconciliation Commission similar to that set up in South Africa at the end of the apartheid era should be established so that non-native Canadians will hear the full story of abuse which might otherwise only be told piecemeal in court.

The failure of pastoral care on the part of church leadership has once more been tragically demonstrated in the stubborn resistance on the part of the Catholic Church to accept its responsibility to compensate native children who were victims of priests and religious in Catholic residential schools in Canada. Although individual religious orders have apologized and paid compensation, the Catholic Church continues to deny its corporate responsibility. The Order of Mary Immaculate (O.M.I.) and the Jesuits have issued apologies for particular instances of abuse, but a public national apology on the part of the Catholic Church has not yet been forthcoming.

The churches have claimed that because they were only administering the schools on behalf of the Canadian government, it should be the government that bears the brunt of the financial burden of the claims. But in 1998, the British Columbia Supreme Court ruled that the churches, even though they had been mandated to administer the schools in the name of the government, were vicariously liable for past abuses committed by their members. Another B.C. Supreme Court judgment apportioned the costs to be born as 60 percent by the churches and 40 percent by the government. The legal costs to the churches have been high: both the United Church and the Anglican Church have spent millions of dollars, and the Anglican Diocese of Cariboo in northern Canada has been forced to close on account of bankruptcy. Now more than seven thousand lawsuits have been filed against the churches, which have been named by the government of Canada as third-party defendants in the cases.

At the time of this writing, there is an impasse in negotiations between the churches and the government. The Anglican Church has withdrawn from the ecumenical group in order to expedite a settlement and avoid continued litigation and further bankruptcies. The Catholic Church is fighting a slick legal campaign to prevent its assets from being forfeited to pay compensation. Lawyers representing the corporate Catholic Church have come up with an ingenious claim. There is no headquarters of the Catholic Church in Canada or worldwide, they argue, no central assets, no central authority responsible for the operation of local churches. Legally the Catholic Church exists as a network of independent episcopal corporations. According to this interpretation of the law, one Catholic diocese is not linked to another Catholic diocese, nor are any of them joined in communion with Rome.[33] This means that each parish in which a residential school was located can declare bankruptcy (and therefore be relieved of any outstanding claims), independent of all the others. The government would then be obliged to come to the rescue and pay the outstanding claims against the church. A series of bankruptcies in small rural parishes would thus not affect the church's central assets, neither would the Vatican be obliged to give financial aid to the Canadian church.

The smugness of this convenient legal fiction disguises a Machiavellian evasion of the church's responsibility. Of all the churches that

were involved in the residential schools, the Catholic Church has the
most to lose because of the number of claims against it. But given
the reach of its global wealth and assets, it is undoubtedly in the best
position to pay. A national poll conducted by the Angus Reid Group
and released in May 2000 suggests that the majority of Canadians
have a different sense of fairness toward the claimants. They believe
that both churches and government should pay the cost for abuse
settlements. They also believe that all Canadians bear some responsibility for the fate of aboriginal peoples.[34] A majority (77 percent)
believes the Catholic Church is well equipped to pay and that the
whole church should shoulder the burden of compensation. This is
a fascinating testament to the fact that, in the mind of the Canadian
public in general, Gil Bailie's analysis of the impact of the life and
teaching of Jesus is true. The victims have indeed assumed the center
stage and the justice of their cause has been widely acknowledged.
It represents an extraordinary reversal of public values and one that
has taken place relatively swiftly, over the past fifty years. It is a terrible irony that those who are most blind to this are the leaders of
the Catholic Church.

The missionaries and administrators who staffed the residential
schools were no different than their contemporaries. The average
white Canadian of the time held derogatory views of native religion
and culture. Christianity was part of the dominant European white
culture imposed by force on North and South America by the missionaries, military personnel, and merchants who flooded to the New
World in the wake of Christopher Columbus and Jacques Cartier. The
forcible assimilation of aboriginal peoples was viewed as a positive
step that would contribute to their ability to function in the dominant society. Most Canadians now view this in hindsight as a grave
mistake. This is a clear indication of the contribution of postmodern
thought, which can deconstruct a hitherto dominant worldview and
introduce a new interpretation of history viewed from the perspective of its victims. It is also a call to the Catholic Church to examine
its traditional policy of forging alliances with powerful and violently
repressive governments in order to facilitate the spread of the gospel.

The fate of the survivors of residential schools is an example of
what the Second Vatican Council named as a "sign of the times."
The realization of the long-term effects of the suffering imposed by
those acting in the name of the various Christian churches has resulted in a moment of crisis for the church, which could also prove

to be an opportunity. That the voices of the victims of the church have now come into speech is a blessing in disguise. Their painful testimony could serve to put an end to the deceits that masquerade as truth in the service of power and bring about a conversion that can restore the church to integrity. Many members of the Anglican Church have come to this realization. "To speak one's sorrow, to speak of one's shame for wrongs committed to aboriginal peoples," wrote Michael Peers, the primate of the Anglican Church of Canada, "is about speaking the truth. The truth does set us free, and refusal to speak it would make impossible the journey of healing that we seek to continue."[35] The worldly assets of the Christian churches may be on the decline as a result of the scandals, but even this could prove to be a blessing in disguise. The large compensation payments, the loss of properties and assets: could all of this not be the Holy Spirit's way of coaxing the church away from a dependence on substantial bank accounts and temporal assets to secure its power?

In a related series of exposures of abuse on the part of Catholic-run institutions in Canada, a dispute over the fate of a group of people known collectively as the Duplessis orphans has surfaced to haunt the Catholic Church and the government in the province of Quebec. Maurice Duplessis, the premier of Quebec in the 1940s and 1950s, ruled the province as a virtual theocracy. Outside of the city of Montreal, most of the province's inhabitants lived in poverty. It was an era when children born out of wedlock were classified as "children of sin." Some children were given to orphanages because their parents were too poor to look after the large families which were the result of the strictly enforced Catholic ban on birth control.

Once placed in Catholic orphanages, the children were arbitrarily pronounced to be "severely retarded" in order that the institutions could qualify for government support. Some three thousand of them spent their childhood and adolescence in horrific conditions where beatings, straitjackets, solitary confinement, and the administration of heavy doses of tranquilizers were common practice. About one thousand of the orphans have survived to middle age. A high suicide rate has claimed many in the group, while others live with severe mental illness and depression.

Now the Duplessis orphans are seeking redress by way of an apology from the church and compensation from both the church and the government. But the church denies it was responsible for classifying the orphans as mentally ill, placing the entire responsibility for the abuse on the shoulders of the Quebec government and its doctors. Quebec's senior prelate, Cardinal Jean-Claude Turcotte of Montreal, has refused to apologize to the orphans, stating that this would denigrate the work of the nuns and monks who ran the institutions. "An apology would be a betrayal of the religious orders," added Bishop Pierre Morissette of Baie-Comeau, then chair of the Assembly of Quebec bishops.[36] Turcotte has also stated that "the orphans don't deserve an apology.... They are victims of life."[37]

The government of the Province of Quebec, however, did apologize to the orphans in 1999. The then premier, Lucien Bouchard, refused individual compensation for the survivors, offering instead to set up a $2 million treatment fund for collective treatment and healing. The provincial ombudsman had recommended $25 million. The orphans rejected Bouchard's offer.

THE SHOCKING IMPACT of the evidence of extensive patterns of sexual and physical abuse of children by priests and nuns placed in positions of trust over them has rippled through the "old" Catholic churches of Europe, North America, and elsewhere. But conservative Catholics, including spokesmen for the Vatican, view this as an indication that the churches in the West have fallen prey to the hedonism and decadence of modern secular society. To them, sexual abuse by priests should be treated as an individual rather than a systemic problem. Catholic priests have simply fallen prey to the temptation to sexual sin so prevalent in the society around them. The churches of the developing world, Africa in particular, are lauded by Rome as youthful, energetic, dynamic, and dedicated, in stark contrast to the flagging churches of the West. It helps that their members are also less likely to criticize Vatican policies. With scores of young aspirants to the priesthood and religious life who have not been corrupted by materialism, feminism, or cynicism they are viewed as the hope of the future of the church. In early 2001, the Catholic Church was rudely awakened from this delusion.

In March 2001 the U.S. *National Catholic Reporter* carried a lead article entitled "Reports of Abuse."[38] The writers summarized three reports that have been presented to the Vatican during the period from 1994 to 2001, outlining evidence of the rape and sexual abuse of nuns by priests. The situation was first brought to the Vatican's attention in a 1994 report by Sr. Maura O'Donohue, who was then the AIDS coordinator for the London-based CAFOD (Catholic Fund for

Overseas Development). Based on evidence culled over a six-year period from fourteen countries in Africa as well as the Philippines, India, Ireland, the United States, and several countries in Latin America, the report documents a situation that demonstrates another example of the denial and subterfuge at the heart of the church.

In parts of the developing world, some Catholic priests exploit their spiritual status and financial superiority to obtain sexual favors from nuns. The abuse has occurred in social contexts where women are culturally conditioned to show subservience toward men. The residential schools offered clergy a context where their superior racial and class identity could be abused. In parts of the developing world, unequal class and gender relations between men and women provide another context for exploitation and abuse by clergy. The women in this instance have been doubly victimized, growing up within a Catholic culture where their school and family education have lacked all but a rudimentary instruction on sex.

In many parts of the developing world, there is a wide gap between the education of priests and that of nuns. Some priests have used this to their advantage. A priest from Tanzania would apparently tell the young nuns whom he was teaching in the novitiate that the Holy Ghost would be visiting their dormitory each night so they should leave the door unlocked. Sure enough, the priest would appear in a long white robe and take one novice each night for "communion" in the form of sexual intercourse.[39] In her 1998 report, Sr. Marie McDonald, Superior General of the Missionary Sisters of Our Lady of Africa, states that "sexual harassment and even rape of sisters by priests and bishops is common... and sometimes when a sister becomes pregnant, the priest insists she have an abortion." O'Donohue's report describes an incident where a priest who took a nun for an abortion, which resulted in her death, then presided at her funeral.

Another factor is the prevalence of HIV/AIDS in parts of the world, especially in Sub-Saharan Africa. This makes women who are vowed to perpetual chastity and sequestered from day-to-day contact with men a safer and more desirable target for sexual activity. "Sadly, the sisters also report that priests have sexually exploited them because they too had come to fear contamination with HIV by sexual contact with prostitutes and other 'at risk' women."[40]

What has been the church's response to these allegations? It has followed the all-too-familiar pattern of dismissing the allegations and punishing the whistleblowers. The entire leadership team of a diocesan women's congregation in Malawi was dismissed by their bishop after they reported to him that priests in the diocese had made twenty-nine nuns pregnant. Another factor that compounds the difficulty of dealing with abuse by priests is that there are no structures within the church to allow lay people who are aware of what is going on to speak out. "Some priests are known to have relationships with several women and also to have children from more than one liaison. Lay people spoke with me about their concerns, saying they are waiting for the day when they will have dialogue homilies. This will afford them an opportunity to challenge certain priests on the sincerity of their preaching and their apparent double standards."[41] A very similar point was made in the Winter Commission Report. "From the laity, the Commission heard constant reference to the power of the priests and to the unquestioning 'blind' obedience given to them in all things. . . . Lay persons had no effective vehicle for criticisms of priests . . . and priests and people rarely share hopes and dreams for the Christian community."[42]

The reaction of Catholic bishops in Africa to these situations of abuse has been similar to the way their brothers elsewhere in the church have treated priests who abused children. The offenders are sent on retreat and then relocated. Priests who have made nuns pregnant "are often only moved to another parish — or sent for studies."[43] Thus reempowered, they are able to continue in priestly ministry. The nuns, however, face a whole series of sanctions. Those who give birth face dismissal from their order. They return to their families "stigmatized and often in very poor economic circumstances. I was given examples in several countries where such women were forced into becoming a second or third wife in a family because of lost status in the local culture."[44]

Because their complaints had been dismissed and had even provoked sanctions from their bishops, some of the women's superiors at the local level approached the superiors of international women's religious orders in Africa that had direct links with the Vatican. It was these other women in leadership positions who took up the cause of the African sisters by filing reports at their international headquarters in Rome. To their consternation, they found that their intervention provoked another round of retaliation against the African sisters. "The bishops felt it was disloyal of the sisters to have sent such reports outside their dioceses." McDonald wrote in her report.[45] "They said that the sisters in question should go to their diocesan bishop with these problems.... The sisters claim they have done so time and time again.... In some cases they are blamed for the problem.... Even when they are listened to sympathetically, nothing much seems to be done."[46]

One priest did speak out about this situation at the time when the first report by O'Donohue was sent to Rome. Fr. Robert de Vitillo, a former director of CARITAS, an overseas development agency of the U.S. bishops, made this observation in a talk he gave at Boston College in 1994. "Religious women have been targeted by clergy who may have previously frequented prostitutes.... Attempts to raise these issues with local and international church authorities have met with deaf ears. In North America and Europe our church is already reeling under the pedophilia scandals. How long will it take for this same institutional church to become sensitive to these new abuse issues which are resulting from the pandemic?"[47]

Rome has finally responded, but not with sensitivity. In what appears to be yet another attempt to brush off the seriousness of this situation, one that has been reported from twenty-three countries, the Vatican's public relations officer, Joaquín Navarro-Valls, admitted that the reports had been received but stated that according to Rome the problem is minor. "The problem is known and it involves a restricted geographical area. Certain negative situations," he added, "must not overshadow the often heroic faith of the overwhelming majority of religious nuns and priests."[48] In May 2001, no less a body than the European Parliament passed an unprecedented motion of condemnation of the Vatican's failure to take action in response to the reports. It recommended that the perpetrators be arrested and handed over to justice.[49] The issue surfaced again at the Synod of Bishops, which met in Rome in October 2001. Some superiors of religious communities of women who were present at the synod addressed the meeting. One of them, Sr. Mary Sujita Kallupurakkathu, superior general of the Sisters of Notre Dame in India, called for the establishment of "a redressal forum to deal firmly and fairly with the increasing experiences of exploitation and abuses of women in general and women religious in particular."[50]

It is sad irony that the very feminism that has become a target of papal condemnation and virulent opposition from right-wing Catholic movements could have helped prevent this major cause of scandal to the church. Frequent Vatican interventions at the United Nations over the past fifteen years have delayed the progress of women, especially in the developing world, to full equality. Exposure to the feminist analysis of gender as a social construct, which the pope so roundly condemns, would have assisted the nuns who were and are being abused by priests. It would have enabled them to understand that fundamental Christian principle that women have the same infinite value in the eyes of God as men and that it is not God's will for them to be subservient to men. Feminist analysis of the Bible, culture, religion, and social status would have helped them to see the historical roots of female subordination, constructed over centuries of male dominance and now being slowly and painfully deconstructed. Feminism would have provided these women with the tools to analyze, critique, and resist the deceitful arguments used by many priests in the process of seducing them.

In July 2001 a group comprised of international Catholic and secular organizations presented a "Call to Accountability" at the Permanent Mission of the Holy See to the United Nations. More than three hundred Catholic and secular organizations worldwide had signed a petition calling on the Vatican to make a public apology for the abuse; to provide counseling, financial support, and therapeutic services for the victims; to reinstate nuns dismissed from their orders; to adopt a policy on sexual conduct aimed at eliminating violence against women; and to cooperate with civil authorities in the prosecution of priests who are guilty of rape.[51] Archbishop Renato Martino, the Vatican's representative at the UN, declined to receive this petition and refused to meet with the organizers. In his letter declining the request, he asked for continuing prayers for the priests involved. His letter contained not a word about their victims. "We [women] are so invisible," commented Frances Kissling, president of Catholics for a Free Choice, one of the groups supporting the petition, "that it doesn't even occur to him to ask for prayers for the victims."[52] While Martino's letter does not rank as an official church document, the lack of sensitivity evident in the nuncio's reaction to the petition speaks volumes about the lack of pastoral sympathy for vulnerable children and women on the part of church's leaders. The plight of the victim does not seem to come within the orbit of their thinking.

THE CATHOLIC CHURCH has tried to cover up the sexual abuse of children by priests and has resisted the calls for change in its structures for fear that this too would cause a loss of face and lead to a decline in its influence. The opposite has in fact happened. So profound has been the loss of the church's credibility in, for example, the formerly Catholic stronghold of Newfoundland, that when that province held a referendum on continued government funding for Catholic schools in 1998, the majority of the population voted in favor of abolishing the Catholic school system altogether.

But what of the majority of Catholic priests, who are neither abusers nor fervent apologists for the present system? Often stretched beyond capacity because of increasing demands, sometimes the targets of the anger of the laity yet always expected to defend the system, many priests these days find themselves caught between the proverbial rock and a hard place. Fr. Donald Cozzens, author of *The Changing Face of the Catholic Priesthood,* subtitled his book "A Reflection on the Priest's Crisis of Soul." "The post-conciliar years," he writes, "have tested the mettle of priests — crisis after crisis 'shaking their foundations' and turning their lives inside out and upside down."[53] Describing the years since the council in the mystical phrase "the dark night of the soul," Cozzens continues. "For the neo-conservative Catholic, any dark night the priest might be suffering was traced to the Church's infidelity to the pre-conciliar structures that resonated with such surety and clarity amid the social chaos and moral relativity of modernity. For other Catholics, however, and for most priests, I believe the dark night was the work of the Spirit, leading priests through dark valleys to a point where they could see new horizons. The darkness was necessary to bring about a conversion of mind and heart, to effect a new way of seeing and listening, an *aggiornamento.*"[54]

This movement, this dark night of the soul, has been shared by the victims of clerical sexual abuse. The breakdown that is taking place in the church is part of the Spirit's work of preparing the ground for the major changes that are inevitable. The pain of the system's victims and the pain of the system's priests are pulling the church toward a new horizon, if those in authority would but look up and see it. The Winter Commission Report states unequivocally that sexual abuse is not just the problem of a few aberrant individuals within the priesthood but a symptom of systemic problems in the church. Its causes inhere within the power structure of the church, a structure that must change if the Catholic Church is to regain its integrity.

One of the flashpoints of controversy over a more systemic change in the church that lurks just below the surface of discussion of sexual abuse by clergy is the issue of compulsory celibacy. The idea of voluntary celibacy as an ascetic practice to substitute for martyrdom dates back to the fourth century when the Roman persecution of Christians ceased. Jesus himself did not advocate or require it of his followers. It was not until the twelfth century that celibacy became a prerequisite for priestly ordination. Four hundred years later, the Protestant Reformers abolished it within the new communities of faith. It has never been imposed on priests in the Orthodox tradition.

So it is the Roman Catholic Church alone which, in the latter half of its history, has clung to a minority view on the necessity of celibacy for ministry. According to the Winter Commission Report, "Much concern has been expressed over the possible link between priestly celibacy . . . and the occurrence of child sexual abuse."[55] The commission states that there is no direct correlation between the two. But in the light of the level of concern expressed by priests and others who were interviewed by the commission, "The Commission concludes that celibacy as an absolute requirement for the ministerial priesthood must be more fully examined by bishops, and that for some individuals it may create excessive and destructive pressure." Sr. Marie McDonald cites similar concerns in her 1998 report on the abuse of African Religious.[56] One of the causes of abuse that she lists is that "Celibacy/Chastity is not a value in many countries."

The evidence of the sexual relationships of Catholic priests with women, particularly women in vulnerable situations, is also part of the general scenario in the breakdown of the observance of compulsory celibacy. In the 1990s, no fewer than seven Catholic bishops resigned because of their difficulties with mandatory celibacy. Bishops Hansjorg Vogel of Basle, Switzerland (1995), and Roderick Wright of Argyll and the Isles (1996) resigned in order to marry. Bishop Eugene Marino of Atlanta resigned in 1990 when his affair with singer Vicki Long was brought to light. Bishop George Patrick Ziemann of Santa Rosa, California, resigned in 1999 after Fr. Jorge Salas, with whom he had had sex for two years in exchange for keeping quiet about Ziemann's thefts of diocesan money, went public. Bishop Hubert O'Connor of Prince George, British Columbia (1991), and Bishop John Ward of Cardiff, Wales (2001), were forced out by revelations of sexual relationships with children and young girls. Other bishops are also currently under investigation.

There is incontrovertible evidence of the negative effects of celibacy, not only through the sexual abuse of children, but also in the significant numbers of priests and bishops who are in covert relationships. All this comes to light at a time when Catholic opinion supports changes in the priesthood, to open it to married men and to women. The church does not move and change with every whim or fluctuation in public opinion, but at the same time there is an ancient tradition which respects the wisdom of the people. As Vatican II stated: "The Holy People of God shares in Christ's prophetic office: it spreads abroad a living witness to Christ especially by a life of faith and love. . . . The whole body of the faithful who have an anointing that comes from the Holy One cannot err in matters of belief."[57] The people of God who kneel faithfully in the pews every Sunday at Mass are not blind to the fact that the average age and the level of stress of their pastors are rising. They question why their church continues to demand celibacy for its own priests who are "cradle Catholics," yet welcomes married Anglican clergy with open arms because the latter are opposed to the ordination of women. They wonder why, in view of the evident crisis which shows no sign of abating, that church authorities stubbornly refuse to admit that it is their hearts that need to be converted and their ears that need to be open to the voice of the Spirit speaking through the signs of the times.

Catholics look to the leaders of their faith community for evidence that they at least make an effort to practice the human rights, compassion, and inclusiveness that they preach to the rest of the world. In the light of Rome's constant admonishments to Catholic laity and to the world in general about sexual conduct, Catholics have the right to expect church leaders to be scrupulously honest and concerned about sexual abuse when it occurs in their own backyard. This is not to say that lay people expect priests and bishops to be perfect. But when the conduct of the clergy reflects a glaring contradiction to the values of the gospel, when bishops defend priests who defile the innocence of children and do not see the necessity for apology or amendment, then widespread cynicism will be the result.

The denial, cover-up, and lying about sexual abuse in the church is a stark demonstration of how the Catholic Church has wandered far from its origins and strayed down a path of internal division between the powerful and the powerless within the institution. The powerful — the pope, bishops, and clergy who claim to have all the truth — have chosen to defend their stunted version of truth, even in the face of repeated evidence that it is corrupt and toxic to the

church's most vulnerable members, children and women. The powerless, the victims of the church, have no voice, no rights, no internal
mechanisms or structure within which they can call the institution to
account. These people have been forced by the church's intransigence
to go outside the church to seek justice, to clamor on the streets of
cities or walk in protest in cathedral precincts, or to have recourse to
secular courts for a just and impartial hearing.

THE INTEGRITY OF THE CHURCH as a community of reconciliation,
the sacrament of God's healing presence on earth, is now at stake.
Sexual abuse arose out of the false culture of domination that the
church has assimilated into its internal structures over the course of
centuries. This culture of domination is exacerbated in the church by
the official promotion of right-wing sects, which preach unquestioning obedience to authority. This has led to a harsh, rigid, and violent
propagation of a version of "truth." The ruling clerical class in the
church has succumbed to the hypnotic, mimetic culture of violence.
Unwilling to face the need for reform that will strip away the power
it has accumulated over years of imposing conformity, it has fallen
into an idolatrous cult of power. Instead of focusing on the decadent
structures of the church which have led to the deceit and denial of
abuse, its leaders have tried to shift the blame onto external targets.
First of all, they blamed the victims for being an "occasion of sin"
for the clergy. Then they blamed the media for causing the crisis by
exposing it to public scrutiny. Then they have tried to downplay the
extent of the crisis, to deal with it in a piecemeal fashion through
local settlements and, most recently, cover it with the veil of secrecy
within the Vatican courts.

The Second Vatican Council introduced concepts of consent, collegiality, and dialogue into Catholic ecclesiology. All of these new
paradigms could, if implemented, have led to a deconstruction of the
power of the Catholic hierarchy. But so tentative were these efforts,
so restricted by traditional language, that the impetus for reform and
any newly found voice of the People of God quickly faltered with the
failure of nerve after the council and during the pontificate of Paul VI.
The process of backtracking from the council has accelerated under
John Paul II. Reactionary forces in the church, as has been seen in
previous chapters, have once again gained the upper hand, and the
energy for reform has all but dissipated. The "restoration" church
of John Paul II has closed its ears to the prompting of the Spirit

unleashed at Vatican II, and the impetus for reform from above has all but ceased.

The Spirit is speaking to the church again. This time it is not from above but from below. The voice of the Spirit cannot be quenched (1 Thess. 5:12). The thrust of reform initiated from above has stalled but the Spirit is pursuing its cause with greater urgency through the cries of the church's own victims. The power structure of the church has failed to reform itself. But with the continuing revelations of clerical abuse, the financial fallout from court settlements, and the resulting erosion of public trust, the hierarchical church is slowly but surely imploding from within. Its eventual collapse and renewal will come all the more suddenly and will be astonishing for those who have not discerned all along the still small voice of the Spirit, even as Rome continues to vaunt the virtues of the present system.

The voices of the church's victims are preaching a redemptive truth that must be listened to if the idolatry of power in the church is to be overcome. These voices from the margins, from the edge, are deconstructing and purifying the church of its worldly attachments and calling it to conversion. If in the process it is purged of its assets, so be it. The fundamental message that runs through the gospel is that the Christian community exists for the sake of the world, not as an end in itself. The mission of the church is to preach the gospel by word and example and to live the truth of the message it teaches.

Three of the gospels record an incident where Jesus was walking through a wheat field on the Sabbath (Mark 2:23–28; Matt. 12:1–8; Luke 6:1–5). His followers began to pick off the heads of wheat and munch on them. The Pharisees were watching closely, and they upbraided him because this violated the law of the Sabbath. That postmodern, peripatetic Jesus answered them with an even stronger example of breaking the rules. He cited with approval the story of David, who was traveling on campaign with a band of soldiers who became hungry. They went right into the sanctuary and ate the consecrated bread, which had been set aside for God and was destined to pass only through the holy hands and mouths of priests (1 Sam. 21). An equivalent scenario today would be if a hungry street person were to go into a Catholic Church, break open the tabernacle, and eat the consecrated hosts reserved inside. Priests and bishop would react with horror, and the church in question would probably be closed and reconsecrated. But "the Sabbath is made for humanity," concluded Jesus, "not humanity for the Sabbath."

The fact that this incident is recorded in three gospels highlights its authenticity and importance for the earliest Christian community. It indicates to the community that the rules are malleable. Boundaries of inclusion and exclusion can be transgressed, especially in favor of the marginalized, who are at the center of the church's concern. If the people are hungry for bodily or spiritual nourishment, they must take it if necessary by stepping across the boundaries laid down by the lawmakers. The clerical structure of the Catholic Church, from the Vatican to the parish, appears to be incapable of reforming itself, even in the face of incontrovertible evidence that these structures have irreparably damaged many Catholic children. The laity, the majority of whom are not members of authoritarian Catholic movements, must act to protect children and demand the necessary reforms. Even that most sacred place, the Holy of Holies, exists to serve the needs of the people. Jesus walks through a cornfield, eats on the Sabbath, and uses this as a way of teaching people about God's priorities. This is a pattern the church needs to readopt. It is time to take the truth back from the temple and out into the fields.

SIX

God in Us and God in All

The Rev. Debbie Little is the Episcopalian pastor at the Common Cathedral in Boston, Massachusetts. She grew up in a middle-class suburb of Boston, and by 1990 she was at the peak of a successful career as communications director at Harvard University's Kennedy School of Management. Debbie had been a student activist in the 1960s. Since then she had become involved in various volunteer activities but, in her own words, "I had a nagging, growing, scary feeling that I wasn't doing what I was meant to do."

So she embarked on a degree in theology at Harvard Divinity School and applied for ordination to the priesthood. Right from the outset of her studies in preparation for ordination, Debbie insisted that her ministry was not to be in a cathedral or a parish, but on the street. "I needed," she explained later, to "be somewhere where the church isn't even sure it belongs." The street did indeed prove to be a controversial place for priestly ministry, and Little's ordination was initially delayed for several months after she finished her studies while the bishop studied the implications of her request.

She was eventually ordained in 1995 at age fifty. She celebrated her first Eucharist at a table in the waiting room at Boston railway station. Then she set out to meet and gather street people on the Boston Common. Armed with a knapsack full of sandwiches, socks, prayer book, and oils for anointing, she began to hang out in the park. After the first two people she talked to spoke to her about God and inquired about her well-being, she began to realize that she was not bringing God to the streets, but discovering the God who was already there.

Her first Eucharist at the street people's fountain on Boston Common drew sixteen people. The altar was a cart used to stack folding chairs that she had wheeled over the street from the nearby cathedral. "I was worried about what the bishop might say about the service," said Debbie, "and our being outdoors...whether I was in some serious error. I was also worried about the park and municipal authorities, since I was sure there must be laws against such gatherings."

"There must be laws against such gatherings." Somehow that sounds familiar. How many times was Jesus chased out of the temple for bringing the wrong people into holy places? People like women, the disabled, the blind, hookers, tax collectors, and others whom religious people judged as outside the borders of God's kindom.

Now the boundaries of the church in Boston have been extended to the street, and the Common Cathedral draws an average of 150 every Sunday. Members of the Common's congregation have started to seek out and to visit other homeless people in the city's hospitals. Street people have also told Debbie that they now feel safer in a shelter when they recognize another member of the Common Cathedral there.

This church of the people that is preaching the good news to the poor is also converting the rest of the church. The movement of the Spirit is propelling the church into places where it is not sure it belongs. Now the bishop and many of the cathedral clergy often come across the street to worship at the Common Cathedral. The Christ who was born outside in the stable and as an adult had no place to lay his head is once more inviting his followers to come and discover where he dwells. Jesus, who celebrated the first Eucharist in a home, is inviting the church to view the whole world as a sacred space. Rather than have God and the world squeezed into the church's rigid boundaries, God is moving to make all previous boundaries fluid.

I participated in Debbie Little's Common Cathedral Eucharist in the fall of 2001. Shortly after, I came across a text that describes the earliest Christian community. It was written in 125 C.E., less than a hundred years after Jesus' death and resurrection.

They walk in all humility and kindness, and falsehood is not found among them, and they love one another. They despise not the widow and grieve not the orphan. Anyone who has distributes liberally to those who have not. If they see any strangers, they bring them under their roof and rejoice over them as though they belonged to their own family: for they call themselves brothers and sisters, not after the flesh, but after the Spirit of God. But when one of the poor passes away from this world and any of them see him, then they provide for his burial according to their ability; and if they hear that any of their number is imprisoned or oppressed for the name of their Messiah, all of them provide for his or her needs. And if it is possible to deliver them, they will do it. Any if there is among them anyone who is poor or needy and they themselves do not have an abundance of necessities, then they will fast for two or three days so that they can provide the needy with the necessary food.[1]

This is the truth, the pattern of Christian practice that we need to take back. It is leaders such as Debbie Little who are showing the way forward for the churches by reclaiming the central traditions of Christianity's origins and interpreting them in the light of the post-modern world. Debbie Little's Common Cathedral is one example among many today where people discover a bridge from the earliest tradition of Christianity to places where God's Spirit of love is at work. In order to construct this bridge, Debbie Little had to confront and then loosen the bonds of power, wealth, and status that have shackled the truth preached by Jesus and hindered the church's witness. In so doing, she has reached back into the earliest ethos of Christianity, before it became engulfed by the empire.

The churches need more such bridge-builders. In the words of feminist theologian Carter Heyward, "Twenty-four hours a day the dominant church and world presses upon us definitions of 'community,' 'justice,' 'love,' 'God,' and 'self' which are exhausting because they are individualistic and adversarial and impossible to embody in healthy and holy ways."[2] It is by abandoning attempts at domination and placing the marginalized at the center, as the first Christians did, that the churches will regain their health. Jesus did not call for his followers to act upon the poor from above, from a higher vantage point of truth, but showed that God's truth is revealed to and through the poor themselves: it is to them, he said, that the secrets of the kingdom are entrusted. We don't bring God to the poor. We find God among the poor.

It requires courage, perseverance, and vision to contend with the church's unhealthy, dysfunctional systems and to start to dismantle them. It is also a lonely road to walk. Prophetic figures like Debbie Little and Carter Heyward exist at the margins of the church and the world. But they are the bridge-builders to the future. To build bridges between Christian tradition and the contemporary world, between different Christian denominations and between Christianity and other religions, between rich and poor, women and men, between humanity and nature: this is the way forward. The future survival of the world lies in establishing new connections, not in maintaining and exacerbating old divisions. It is not possible to re-create the churches *ex nihilo*. But the renewal of the churches requires a deconstruction of false ideologies of power and experimentation with different possibilities. We must reclaim our common ownership of the truth with which the Spirit has endowed us all. God is working powerfully in women and men in our time to take back the truth.

Is GOD REALLY GOD, or is God subject to the boundaries of human definition? The religious context is the final and most resistant boundary to the postmodern critique of the foundations of the great narratives that have sustained past history. The leaders of the Catholic Church and of the religious right are reluctant to face the repressed histories of those, such as women, gays, and lesbians, deemed outside the boundaries of power. At the heart of the planet's future survival lies the reconciliation of all previous opposites.

"Postmodernity may pave the way to letting God be God again,"[3] states theologian David Tracy. In Tracy's view, postmodernity has made it possible to take back God from the stifling embrace of the dominant Christian churches by bringing about the interruption of Western Eurocentric history. This movement has led to a critique of the role of Christianity in establishing the West's colonial systems of oppressive dominance. God is being restored to being God again because it is becoming evident that God can no longer be controlled by small groups of men. The mystery of God is being released from the gilded cages of dogma. God's incomprehensibility is a positive impetus to enter anew into mystery and to experience that God's love is so excessive as to be incomprehensible. Christ's incarnation, death, and resurrection means that in this dangerous and disruptive God-in-Christ we discover the motivation to continue the struggle in history for justice and compassion.

This is a post-Auschwitz God who suffers with the marginalized and whose compassion is beyond all reason. In response to the Holocaust, Elie Wiesel, Dorothee Soelle, and others who have attempted to articulate the mystery of God manifested in the post-Holocaust world have suggested that perhaps God cannot be both all-powerful and all-loving. "Historical events would seem to demonstrate this. . . . Rather than simply concede that God is not all-powerful, it seems spiritually and morally more fully true to reinterpret God's power as the power of love, a power recognizable not by its control but by its vulnerability — that is its openness to being touched and changed by what is happening."[4]

The false notion that the fullness of God's truth and love are still restricted to a chosen elite is being fiercely defended at all levels. The new global aggressiveness of George W. Bush's Republican America is supported by fundamentalist Christians both Catholic and Protestant. The Vatican's fight against women's equality in the church and at the UN is supported by right-wing Protestants and some Islamic theocracies. Militant Islamic movements call for the *jihad* against the corruption of the West that issued in the events of September 11. The current resurgence of fundamentalism and its backlash against the pluralism, democracy, tolerance, and inclusivity of postmodern society could be the last gasp of patriarchal religions before the world comes to a new realization of the need for connectedness. Left unchallenged, however, these right-wing religious movements are set to plunge the world into a frightening new age of global violence and destruction.

The resurgence of religious fundamentalism is in part a sign of the desperation of those who feel threatened by humanity's new step forward into a pluralistic world. Their response is to regress into the past rather than take the risk of going forth into the future. Leaders of fundamentalist religious movements are holding on to old identities and attempting to enforce an old collective ideology. They are attempting to remold these identities by projecting their fear of change onto "the other" and what she or he represents. Religions have manufactured a God in their own image who supports religious sanctions against those who don't fit this image. Their fear is contagious and irrational and, as René Girard has pointed out, it results in violent purges of scapegoats and dissidents. The fear of the power of their own repressed sexuality leads the celibate leadership of the Catholic Church to ban women from touching the sacred vessels and to forbid gays and lesbians in relationships from approaching the communion rails. In several religious communities, the name of God is now once more invoked as a justification of war. In some extreme right-wing anti-choice groups, their religious beliefs provide the justification to kill abortion providers or to intimidate their families.

But we cannot avoid the fundamental questions about God. Is God just for "us" or for everyone? Is God like all of "us," or only like just a few of us? Is God for or against women? Does God hate gays and lesbians?

After September 11, 2001, we also ask ourselves: Is God for or against my enemies? And is my definition of "the enemy" the same as God's definition? Does God even have enemies? Can humanity coexist peacefully in a pluralist world or will we be condemned forever to internecine violence and hate? Can we find ethical commonality and live in peaceful coexistence amid cultural and religious difference? Yes indeed we can, if we recognize that God is in the connections, that God is in our enemies, that God is immanent in all that lives, that God is "both-and" rather than "either-or."

With God's help, we can be restored to wholeness, but only by embracing diversity, not by seeking uniformity. We can no longer survive as warring tribes, only as a collective. The universal is the only reference. Jesus was reaching toward this stage of universal consciousness. It was women — the Canaanite woman and her daughter, the Samaritan woman at the well — who encouraged him to take this crucial step outside his own boundaries. Jesus took back the truths of God's revelation that had been usurped by the guardians of orthodoxy, the Pharisees, and challenged the margins of their definitions. As Gil Bailie observed, "Hyper-scrupulous adherence to received doctrine has led to distortions of the gospel spirit at least as often as doctrinal carelessness."[5] Some of the worst betrayals of the gospel have been motivated by attempts to "save" it.

THE PRESENT BREAKDOWN of institutional Christianity is actually a legacy of the crucifixion. The cross is not about being a winner, but about siding with the victim. It is not about amassing cheering crowds of youths in a stadium and being feted and honored by the leaders of this world, but about walking with homeless youth on the streets and being shunned by the religious and political establishments.

Jesus did not fall back on false dominance to avoid the consequences of his solidarity with the marginalized. In the conversation with Pilate about the nature of truth, he alluded to the fact that he could call down legions of angels to enforce his version of truth, but that is not the way that the God whom Jesus embodied chose to act. Jesus' God does not draw people into transformation through fear, power, and domination but through conviction and love. This is the challenge of taking back the truth and discovering the answer to Pilate's question to Jesus.

Caiaphas, whose name, like that of the first pope, Peter, means Rock,[6] conspired with Pilate to condemn Christ. Caiaphas set Jesus on the road to Calvary because he was afraid that doctrinal mistakes were being made. Caiaphas's efforts to preserve the truth silenced the dissenting voice of Christ. "The challenge of the postmodern situation is to evade every type of thought control and to cultivate a sensitivity for the coincidental, ambivalent, ambiguous, temporal and uncontrolled, without sinking into the complete arbitrariness of political and moral indifference."[7]

The ambiguity, obscurity, and danger of the present moment notwithstanding, I continue to stay engaged in the struggle for truth and justice in the church and in society. The following prayer that I wrote in 1992, shortly after I had spent that night of the Ash Wednesday protest against the Gulf War in jail, explains why.

> I long to be part of a Christian community that is
> Open to the world.
> Rooted in vulnerability, not power.
> Centered in the Spirit of the Risen, Cosmic Christ.
> Where hope, love, and trust in the Spirit cast out fear.
> Where sacraments celebrate the divine milieu of the sacredness
> of the material world.
> Where deep mutual eroticism is released
> in reciprocal empowerment toward right relation.
> Where Wisdom cries aloud in the marketplace
> summoning us to the banquet of the new creation.
> Where we begin to live and die now
> as though God reigned on behalf of the poor.
> Where Catholic means ecumenical, spacious,
> exuberant in diversity, open to other traditions.
> Where poets are honored,
> artists flourish, musicians are celebrated,
> and mystics held in reverence.
> Where in a wilderness of destruction, alienation,
> addiction, and hopelessness,
> the great voice of God cries out,
> calling us to choose LIFE and LOVE over death and hate.

Blueprint for the Next Pope

- Return the church to spiritual rather than political leadership. Restore jurisdiction to bishops at the local level and transform the papacy into a symbol of unity and communion between the churches. Restore synods of bishops, local and international, as the governing bodies of the churches. Abolish the parallel jurisdiction of papal nuncios.

- Abandon Vatican City as a state and move the administration of the Church to St. John Lateran (as suggested by John Paul I). Hand over the Vatican museums and buildings to UNICEF to hold in trust for future generations.

- Offer Vatican City as a site for the United Nations so that it would have a totally independent headquarters. Abolish the Vatican diplomatic service and pare down the curia.

- Implement Pope John Paul's exhortation to bishops and priests to live in poverty. Open up spare spaces in church rectories, convents, and monasteries to the homeless and poor. Encourage all Catholics to do the same in their homes.

- Settle the financial claims of the victims of pedophilia and sexual abuse without further legal prevarication in order to bring closure to this terrible chapter in recent church history. Sacrifice the church's material assets if necessary.

- Alleviate the shortage of priests by inviting married priests and their wives back to active ministry. Start local experimentation with married priests and the ordination of women. Monitor the results to convey them to the church at large.

- Focus the church's energy away from internal bickering over minor points of doctrinal conformity and outward toward the works of love in the world.

- Celebrate the pluralism of theology within the church and engage the critical voices of liberation, feminist, and creation-centered theologies as well as the cultural particularities of Asian and African theologies.

- Encourage a renewal of the diversity in Catholic liturgical tradition. If people want a Tridentine Mass in Latin, let them worship that way.

- Open up theological discussion within the church as a necessary step toward engaging on a wider basis with other religions and society. Acknowledge the limited nature of Roman theology.

- Impose a moratorium on celibate pronouncements on sexual relationships and on clerical statements on women. Convene a synod of lay people elected by local churches all over the world to discuss the church's response to the AIDS crisis.

- Incorporate women's experience into church teaching and encourage the participation of women at all levels in the church. Invite feminist scholars and theologians back into church institutions of learning.

- Celebrate the goodness and fecundity of mutual relationships without insisting on an intrinsic connection between sexuality and procreation. Invite gay men and women to teach the church about homosexual unions.

- Stop all attempts to whitewash the church's past, especially its complicity with Nazism in World War II. Open up all Vatican archives connected with the Holocaust.

- Celebrate the goodness of creation and the communion and connectedness of all life. Modify the teaching on the superiority of the human over the natural world in favor of the stewardship of the human within the natural world.

- Work to change the spirit of pessimism, distrust, and condemnation of contemporary society in the church and replace it with compassion and solidarity as hallmarks of the church's outreach to the world.

Notes

Chapter 1: What Is Truth?

1. The Innu, distinct from Inuit and Indian, are one of Canada's aboriginal peoples. They live a seminomadic life in the forests of Labrador in eastern Canada.

2. See Girard's *Violence and the Sacred* (Baltimore: Johns Hopkins University Press, 1979); *Things Hidden since the Foundation of the World* (Stanford, Calif.: Stanford University Press, 1987); *Job, the Victim of His People* (New York: Crossroad, 1987).

3. "Metanarrative" refers to the foundational myths for so long accepted in Western society that have sustained social relationships based on a hierarchy of class, race, and gender and supported the dominance of white heterosexual men in social and religious institutions.

4. The phrase "hermeneutic of suspicion" refers to the approach utilized by feminist and liberation scholars when dealing with biblical or ecclesiastical texts. Because these texts were written in a patriarchal context, they have been used in the past to advocate and continue the subordination of women and marginalized men. The texts must be approached with caution and carefully scrutinized in order to expose this.

5. See Stanley J. Grenz, *A Primer on Postmodernism* (Grand Rapids: William B. Eerdmans, 1996), 164ff.

6. Ellen Armour, *Deconstruction, Feminist Theology, and the Problem of Difference* (Chicago: University of Chicago Press, 1999), 3.

7. Aloysius Pieris, S.J., *Fire and Water: Basic Issues in Asian Buddhism and Christianity* (Maryknoll, N.Y.: Orbis Books, 1996), 124.

8. "Caesaropapism" refers to a theory articulated by medieval popes such as Innocent III and Boniface VIII that the purpose of the state is to serve the interests of the church.

9. In his public letter of resignation from the priesthood (February 1, 2001), former Missionary of the Sacred Heart Fr. Paul Collins states that the elitist and exclusive mentality now current at the Vatican threatens to change the Catholic Church into a sect.

10. Carl Bernstein and Marco Politi, *His Holiness: John Paul II and the Hidden History of Our Time* (New York: Doubleday, 1996), 526.

11. Rosemary Radford Ruether, "Christianity Gives Family Values a New Spin," *National Catholic Reporter,* December 12, 1997.

Chapter 2: The Deconstruction of Divinity

1. See Carolyn Osiek's analysis in "Commentary on Philippians," in *Searching the Scriptures: A Feminist Commentary,* ed. Elisabeth Schüssler Fiorenza (New York: Crossroad, 1994), 237–49.

2. Ibid., 242.

3. See Rosemary Radford Ruether, *Introducing Redemption in Christian Feminism* (Sheffield, U.K.: Sheffield Academic Press, 1998), 102, where she summarizes the theories of womanist theologian Delores Williams.

4. Paul Ricoeur, *Le Conflit des interpretations: Essais d'hermeneutique* (Paris: Editions du Seuil, 1986), 26.

5. Gil Bailie, *Violence Unveiled: Humanity at the Crossroads* (New York: Crossroad, 1995), 17.

6. The "First Wave of Feminism" generally refers to the struggle for women's suffrage that took place in the late nineteenth and early twentieth centuries. The "Second Wave" began with the women's liberation movement of the 1960s and continued until the 1990s as women struggled for equality of opportunity and access in all spheres of life.

7. Elisabeth Schüssler Fiorenza was the first to coin these phrases in her book *In Memory of Her: A Feminist Theological Reconstruction of Christian Origins* (New York: Crossroad, 1987).

8. See Bailie, *Violence Unveiled.*

9. Phyllis Trible, *Texts of Terror: Literary-Feminist Readings of Biblical Narratives* (Philadelphia: Fortress Press: 1984), 3.

10. See Schüssler Fiorenza, *In Memory of Her,* chapter 5.

11. Bruce Chilton, *Rabbi Jesus: An Intimate Biography* (New York: Doubleday, 2000), 13.

12. René Girard, *Job, the Victim of His People* (New York: Crossroad, 2000), 35.

13. Bailie, *Violence Unveiled,* 24.

14. Ibid., 215.

15. "Kindom" is a word commonly used by feminist theologians to describe the community of God in preference to the more masculine and hierarchical "kingdom."

Chapter 3: The Ambiguous Legacy of John Paul II

1. See Lisa Sowle Cahill, "Feminist Ethics, Differences, and Common Ground," in *Feminist Ethics and the Catholic Moral Tradition,* ed. Charles E. Curran, Margaret A. Farley, and Richard A. McCormick (New York: Paulist Press, 1996), 3.

2. Ellen T. Armour, *Deconstruction, Feminist Theology, and the Problem of Difference* (Chicago: University of Chicago Press, 1999), 87.

3. See the analysis in my first book, *Is the Pope Catholic? A Woman Confronts Her Church* (Toronto: Malcolm Lester Books, 1999).

4. Rocco Buttiglione, *Karol Wojtyla: The Thought of the Man Who Became Pope John Paul II* (Grand Rapids: William B. Eerdmans, 1997), 43–53.

5. Gender-exclusive masculine language is used throughout the encyclical.

6. Canon 1371, Number 1.

7. Nicholas Lash, "Teaching in Crisis," in *Considering Veritatis Splendor,* ed. John Wilkins (Cleveland: Pilgrim Press, 1994), 29.

8. Slavery was initially viewed by popes, such as Gregory I, as part of the natural order established by God. As late as 1866, the church publicly condoned the owning of slaves. Slavery was condemned by Pope Leo XIII in *Rerum Novarum* only in 1891. The charging of interest on loans was unequivocally condemned by the church up until the sixteenth century, when exceptions were gradually introduced. See Maureen

Fiedler and Linda Rabben, *Rome Has Spoken* (New York: Crossroad, 1998), 81–90 and 198–207.

9. Gil Bailie, *Violence Unveiled: Humanity at the Crossroads* (New York: Crossroad, 1995), 274.

10. Josef Fuchs, "Good Acts and Good Persons," in *Considering Veritatis Splendor,* ed. Wilkins, 21ff.

11. Peter de Rosa, *Vicars of Christ* (London: Bantam Press; New York: Crown, 1988), 221ff.

12. Barbara Hilkert Andolsen, "Women in Roman Catholic Sexual Ethics," in *Feminist Ethics and the Catholic Moral Tradition,* 209.

13. René Girard, *Violence and the Sacred* (Baltimore: Johns Hopkins University Press, 1979), chapter 4.

14. Lisa Sowle Cahill, "Accent on the Masculine," in *Considering Veritatis Splendor,* ed. Wilkins, 59.

15. Clifford Longley, "In a Muddle over Abortion," *The Tablet,* June 9, 2001.

16. *http://news.bbc.co.uk/hi/english/world/europe/newid.stm.*

17. Daniel Dombrowski and Robert Deltete, *A Brief Liberal Catholic Defense of Abortion* (Chicago: University of Illinois Press, 2000), 38ff.

18. Catholics for a Free Choice, *A History of Abortion in the Catholic Church* (Washington, D.C.: CFFC, 1999), 25.

19. Dombrowski and Deltete, *A Brief Liberal Catholic Defense of Abortion,* 58.

20. Ibid., 24.

21. Catholics for a Free Choice, *A History of Abortion in the Catholic Church,* 12.

22. Ibid., 13.

23. Sedes Apostolica, *Codex iuris canonici fontes,* ed. Pietro Gasparri (Rome: Typis polyglottis vaticanis, 1923–39), 330–31.

24. Holy Office, 1773, *Collectanea de Propaganda Fidei,* no. 282 (Rome: Vatican Press, 1907), 92; cited in Catholics for a Free Choice, *A History of Abortion in the Catholic Church,* 16.

25. Dombrowski and Deltete, *A Brief Liberal Catholic Defense of Abortion,* 38.

26. Ibid., 57.

27. Jim Castelli, *The Bishops and the Bomb: Waging Peace in a Nuclear Age* (New York: Doubleday, 1983); text of the bishops' 1983 Pastoral is on pp. 185–276.

28. Ibid., 216.

29. Joe Woodward, "Catholic Tory Leader Rebuked for His Pro-abortion Stand," *Calgary Herald,* February 28, 2001.

Chapter 4: The New Catholic and Protestant Religious Right

1. Joanna Manning, *Is the Pope Catholic? A Woman Confronts Her Church* (Toronto: Malcolm Lester Books, 1999).

2. Carter Heyward, *Saving Jesus from Those Who Are Right: Rethinking What It Means to Be Christian* (Minneapolis: Fortress Press, 1999), 14.

3. For a more extensive treatment of their activity at the United Nations, see *Is the Pope Catholic?* chapter 5.

4. *www.eriebenedictines.org.* See also Margot Patterson, "Saying 'No' to the Vatican: Obedience Is a Complex Matter," *National Catholic Reporter,* July 27, 2001, 5.

5. Carl Bernstein, "The Holy Alliance," *Time,* February 24, 1992, 14–21.

6. Dennis Doyle, specialist on the papacy, Ohio University, quoted in Michael Valpy, "Pope Diplomatic in View on War," *Globe and Mail,* October 25, 2001, A3.

7. An anathema is an official condemnation of a doctrinal or moral position which excludes the holder from the religious community.

8. Karen Armstrong, *The Battle for God* (New York: Alfred A. Knopf, 2000), 270.

9. David Chilton, reconstructionist theologian, quoted in Frederic Clarkson, *Eternal Hostility: The Struggle between Theocracy and Democracy* (Monroe, Me.: Common Courage Press, 1997), 97.

10. Clarkson, *Eternal Hostility,* 85.

11. Ibid., 85, quoting from Gary North, *Political Polytheism: The Myth of Pluralism* (Tyler, Tex.: Institute for Christian Economics, 1989).

12. John Allen, "The Vatican's Enforcer," *National Catholic Reporter,* April 16, 1999.

13. Papal Message to the Congregation for the Doctrine of the Faith, January 28, 2000, *www.zenit.org.*

14. Leonardo Boff, "Joseph Cardinal Ratzinger: The Executioner of the Future? A Response to Dominus Jesus," in Koinonia, Servicio Bíblico Latinoamericano. *www.servicioskoinonia.org/relat/233e.htm.*

15. Gregory Baum, "Reflections on Dominus Jesus," *Ecumenist* 37, no. 4 (fall 2000).

16. John Allen, "Battle over Translation Body Reflects Wider Liturgical Wars," *National Catholic Reporter,* December 31, 1999, 5.

17. John Allen, "Bishops Reject Controls Sought by Rome," *National Catholic Reporter,* May 12, 2000, 9.

18. U.S. Conference of Catholic Bishops, at *www.nccbuscc.org/liturgy/current/revmissalisromanien.htm.*

19. Robert Boston, *The Most Dangerous Man in America? Pat Robertson and the Christian Coalition* (New York: Prometheus Books, 1996), 158.

20. Bruce Bawer, *Stealing Jesus: How Fundamentalism Betrays Christianity* (New York: Three Rivers Press, 1997), 221.

21. See *www.thelambsofchrist.com.*

22. "Inside the Secret World of Opus Dei," May 1997, at *http://users.skynet.be/sky73819/opusdei.html.*

23. Richard McBrien, quoting Vladimir Feltzmann, Opus Dei member for twenty-two years, in "Questions Cast Dark Clouds over Opus Dei, Church," *National Catholic Reporter,* February 21, 1992.

24. Michael Walsh, *The Secret World of Opus Dei* (London: Grafton Books, 1989), 110.

25. Ibid., 113.

26. Ibid., 114.

27. Ibid., 119.

28. Opus Dei Constitutions, No. 39. Quoted in Hansard, Debates of the Senate of Canada, September 30, 1986–October 1, 1988, 1152.

29. Walsh, *The Secret World of Opus Dei,* 124.

30. Maria del Carmen Tapia, *Beyond the Threshold: A Life in Opus Dei* (New York: Continuum, 1997), 157.

31. Dr. Clementina Meregalli Anzilotti, "Documenti di Lavoro" (Deila Rondaeione, RUI), Rome, April 1994, in Catholics for a Free Choice, *Conservative Catholic Influence in Europe* (Washington, D.C.: CFFC, 1999), 7.

32. *Prairie Messenger,* May 7, 1997, 4.

33. Catholics for a Free Choice, *Conservative Catholic Influence in Europe,* 4.

34. François Geinoz, text for a lecture on the 1994 Cairo Conference on Population and Development, unpublished manuscript, quoted in ibid., 6.

35. Walsh, *The Secret World of Opus Dei,* 180n.

36. Penny Lernoux, "The Papal Spiderweb-I: Opus Dei and 'The Perfect Society,'" *The Nation,* April 10, 1989.

37. Barbara J. Fraser, "Peru's New Cardinal Known for Standing with the Powerful," *National Catholic Reporter,* March 23, 2001.

38. Zenit News Agency, December 21, 2001, *www.zenit.org.*

39. Centre for Counterintelligence and Security Studies, record of BBC documentary, June 1, 2001, at *http://cicentre.com/DOC_Hannsen_BBC_Documentary.html.*

40. Gil Bailie, *Violence and the Sacred* (New York: Crossroad, 1999), 71.

41. *www.odan.org/questionp.html.*

42. Walsh, *The Secret World of Opus Dei,* 162.

43. Ibid., 163.

44. "They Said What?" *www.knowhow.com/yah/hli.htm.*

45. Paul Marx, *The Flying Monk* (Front Royal, Va.: Human Life International Press, 1990), 22.

46. Paul Marx, *Confessions of a Pro-Life Missionary* (Front Royal, Va.: Human Life International Press, 1988), 268.

47. Ibid., 271–72.

48. G. Montini and E. Cartman, "In the Name of the Fetus": HLI, the Catholic Right, and the Vatican's Crusade for Patriarchy," *http://burn.ucsd.edu/aff,* March 17, 1999.

49. *Ft. Wayne News-Sentinel,* August 16, 1993.

50. Clarkson, *Eternal Hostility,* 90

51. Michele Mandel, "Fanning the Flames of Hatred," *Toronto Sun,* April 4, 1999, 5.

52. Transcript of CBC videotape, *A Time to Kill,* December 13, 1994.

53. *Wanderer,* September 2, 1999.

54. Richard Healy, letter to HLI Board, quoted in the *Wanderer* article, September 2, 1999.

55. Federal Court of Canada, Document A-288-94, *Human Life International in Canada Inc. v. M.N.R. Court of Appeal,* Ottawa, February 4, February 6, and March 18, 1998.

56. Catholics for a Free Choice, *Bad Faith at the UN: Drawing Back the Curtain on the Catholic Family and Human Rights Institute* (Washington, D.C.: CFFC, 2001), 9.

57. Ibid., 10.

58. Austin Ruse, speech to the Cardinal Mindzenty foundation, March 19, 2000, quoted in Catholics for a Free Choice, *Bad Faith at the UN,* 5.

59. Ibid.

60. Ibid.

61. Boston, *The Most Dangerous Man in America?* 145.

62. Ibid., quoting from Pat Robertson, *The New World Order: It Will Change the Way You Live* (Dallas: Word Publishing, 1991), 37.

63. Population Research Institute, "The Barrenness of Success," *www.pop.org/briefings/barreness/html.*

64. *Catholic Register*, September 25, 2000, 24.

65. *The Tablet*, September 29, 2001, 1385.

66. Frank Kools, "Catholicism Threatens Liberal EU," in *Trouw* (The Netherlands), November 29, 2001.

67. Anick Druelle, "Right-Wing, Anti-Feminist Groups at the United Nations," unpublished paper for the Institute for Feminist Studies and Research, University of Montreal, 2000, 15.

68. Ibid., 5.

69. Jennifer Butler, "The Religious Right Goes Global," unpublished paper for the Ecumenical Women 2000+, Ecumenical Women's Alliance, New York, 2000, 2.

70. Ibid., 5.

71. Ibid.

72. *Louisville Courier-Journal*, February 18, 1996.

73. Speech at HLI conference, 1994.

74. Butler, "The Religious Right Goes Global," 7.

75. Angus Reid Organization, poll on religious views of Canadians, reported by Michael Valpy in "The Young Still Believe," *Globe and Mail*, April 22, 2000, A1.

76. Ibid.

77. ABT Associates of Canada, Project Report on Catholic Education in the Separate School System in Ontario, prepared for the Institute for Catholic Education, Toronto, May 1990.

78. Ibid., 82.

79. Ibid., 84.

80. John Fulton, *Young Catholics at the New Millennium: The Religion and Morality of Young Adults in Western Countries* (Dublin: University of Dublin Press, 2001), 102.

Chapter 5: Pedophilia and Sexual Abuse

1. Canadian Press Report, "Minister Wasn't at Meeting on Cashel, Probe Told," *Globe and Mail*, January 23, 1990.

2. Barry M. Coldrey, "Religious Life without Integrity," *www.thelinkup.com/integrity2.html.*

3. Kristen Lombardi, "Failure to Act," *Providence Phoenix News,* October 5, 2001.

4. Michael Rezendes and Globe Spotlight Team, "Church Allowed Abuse by Priest for Years," *Boston Globe,* January 6, 2002.

5. Pam Belluck, "Six Priests Suspended after Claims of Sexual Abuse," *Boston Globe,* February 8, 2002.

6. The other members of the Winter Commission were Frances O'Flaherty, M.S.W.; Sister Nuala P. Kenny, M.D., F.R.C.P. (C); Rev. Everett MacNeil, M.A., J.C.L.; and John A. Scott, Ph.D.

7. *The Report of the Archdiocesan Commission of Enquiry into the Sexual Abuse of Children by Members of the Clergy* (St. John's, Newfoundland: Archdio-

cese of St. John's, 1990), 1:24; commonly referred to as the *Winter Commission Report.*

8. Ibid., 137.

9. Ibid., 138.

10. Ibid., 94.

11. Ibid.

12. Donald Cozzens, *The Changing Face of the Catholic Priesthood* (Collegeville, Minn.: Liturgical Press, 2000), 135.

13. *Winter Commission Report,* 1:95.

14. Ibid., 1:97.

15. Ibid., 1:161.

16. "Convicted Priest Assigned to Church," *Toronto Star,* February 3, 2002, A11.

17. Cozzens, *The Changing Face of the Catholic Priesthood,* 119.

18. *Winter Commission Report,* 1:139.

19. Jason Berry and Gerald Renner, "Sex-Related Case Blocked in Vatican," *National Catholic Reporter,* December 7, 2001.

20. Ibid.

21. Ibid.

22. Margaret Kennedy, "Christianity and Child Sexual Abuse: The Survivors' Voice Leading to Change," *Child Abuse Review* 9 (2000): 124–41.

23. "Church Paid Man $32,000 to Keep Quiet on Sex Abuse," *Toronto Star,* January 13, 1994.

24. "Joe Henley in Paris," *Guardian,* June 14, 2001.

25. Kevin Donovan, "Bishops Hope New Guidelines Will Avert Abuse," *Toronto Star,* February 11, 2001, A14.

26. Simon Lister, Special Report, *Tablet,* October 28, 2000, 1468–69.

27. *www.catholicworldnews.com,* September 7, 2001.

28. John Thavis, "Vatican Takes Control over Pedophilia Cases," *Catholic Register* (Toronto), December 16, 2001, 20.

29. Jane O'Hara, "No Forgiving: Canada's Largest Churches Are Reeling under Litigation Costs Arising out of Their Days Running Native Residential Schools," *Macleans,* June 26, 2000.

30. Royal Commission on Aboriginal Peoples, chapter 10, Government of Canada, 1996, quoted in David Napier, "Sins of the Fathers: The Legacy of Indian Residential Schools," *Supplement to the Anglican Journal,* May 2000.

31. Jane O'Hara, "Abuse of Trust: What Happened behind the Walls of Residential Church Schools Has Left Native Victims Traumatized," *Macleans,* June 26, 2000, 16–21.

32. Lorna Dueck, "Sorry Isn't Good Enough," *Globe and Mail,* October 31, 2000, A21.

33. Scott Simmie, "Churches Reaping Harvest of Residential Sexual Abuse," *Toronto Star,* August 26, 2000, A1–A2.

34. Steven Chase, "Residential-School Costs Should Be Shared, Poll Says," *Globe and Mail,* September 8, 2001.

35. Archbishop Michael Peers, primate of the Anglican Church of Canada, sermon at St. James' Cathedral, September 25, 2000, reported in the Comment section, *Globe and Mail,* September 26, 2000, A11.

36. Campbell Clark, "Duplessis Orphans Get No Apology, Compensation," *National Post*, September 16, 1999, 12.

37. Colin Nickerson, "Duplessis Orphans," *Boston Globe,* March 28, 2000.

38. John L. Allen Jr. and Pamela Schaeffer, "Reports of Abuse: AIDS Exacerbates Exploitation of Nuns Reports Allege," *National Catholic Reporter,* March 16, 2001.

39. Ohio Religious Coalition, " A Call to Action from Member Organizations," *Report from Spring Forum,* March 28, 2001.

40. Allen and Schaeffer, "Reports of Abuse," 2.

41. Ibid., 6.

42. *Winter Commission Report,* 1:102–3.

43. Allen and Schaeffer, "Reports of Abuse," 4.

44. Ibid., 6.

45. Ibid., 8.

46. Ibid.

47. "Theological Challenges Posed by the Global Pandemic of HIV/AIDS," *National Catholic Reporter,* March 16, 2001, 5.

48. Stephanie Flanders, "Sexual Abuse of Nuns by Priests Is Protested," *New York Times,* July 15, 2001.

49. *European Parliament Resolution on Sexual Violence against Women, Particularly Catholic Nuns,* B5-026, 0272,0280 and 0298/2001, adopted April 5, 2001.

50. John L. Allen Jr., "Issue of Sexual Abuse of Nuns by Priests Raised at Synod," *National Catholic Reporter,* October 26, 2001.

51. *www.calltoaccountability.org.*

52. Angela Bonavoglia, "Groups Target Abuses by Clergy," *Chicago Tribune,* July 18, 2001.

53. Cozzens, *The Changing Face of the Catholic Priesthood,* 130.

54. Ibid.

55. *Winter Commission Report,* 1:97.

56. Allen and Schaeffer, "Reports of Abuse," 5.

57. *Lumen Gentium,* chapter 2, paragraph 12, in *The Conciliar and Post Conciliar Documents,* ed. Austin Flannery (Boston: St. Paul Editions, 1980), 363.

Chapter 6: Let Go and Let God

1. *The Writings of the Christian Philosopher Aristides,* quoted in *Simpler Living, Compassionate Life: A Christian Perspective,* ed. Michael Schut (Denver: Living the Good News, 1999), 151.

2. Carter Heyward, *Saving Jesus from Those Who Are Right: Rethinking What It Means to Be Christian* (Minneapolis: Fortress Press, 1999), 199.

3. David Tracy, *On Naming the Present: God, Hermeneutics, and the Church* (Maryknoll, N.Y.: Orbis Books, 1994), 37.

4. Heyward, *Saving Jesus from Those Who Are Right,* 155.

5. Gil Bailie, *Violence Unveiled: Humanity at the Crossroads* (New York: Crossroad, 1995), 174.

6. Bruce Chilton, *Rabbi Jesus: An Intimate Biography* (New York: Doubleday, 2000), 302.

7. Annelies Van Heijst, *Longing for the Fall* (Kampen, The Netherlands: Kok Pharos, 1995), 24.

Index